Guitar Mastery Simplified

How **<u>Anyone</u>** Can Quickly Become a Strumming, Chords, and Lead Guitar Ninja

By: Erich Andreas

ISBN: 978-1482650105

Terms of Use

You are given a non-transferable, "personal use" license to this product. You cannot distribute it or share it with other individuals.

Also, there are no resale rights or private label rights granted when purchasing this document. In other words, it's for your own personal use only.

Table of Contents

Quick Summary

Chapters 1 through 3 will get you acclimated to your guitar and prepare you for what we plan on accomplishing in this book. Basically it's our warm-up! But don't skip it! There are reasons why athletes warm up before a big game!

Chapters 4 through 10 are the core lessons that will carry you the furthest with your guitar playing. They cover foundational principles that are paramount to being able to play a LOT of songs in a short amount of time. They will answer the how's and why's to solid "core" playing. They are also often times the lessons that are NOT taught by guitar teachers, either because those teachers have not taken the time to develop their curriculum, or they don't want to take the necessary time developing these fundamental skills in their students.

Chapters 11 through 29 focus on further developing the core that we learned in chapters 4 through 10. You will learn a lot of "ninja" tricks to better comprehend the fret board. You will understand when and how to play further up the neck. You will be introduced to scales and fret board maps that will FINALLY unlock the mystery of the guitar to you.

Learning guitar is a step-by-step process. The reason that so many students have started learning the guitar and then quit was because of an incorrect order of steps and/or not enough time developing those core steps.

This book is different. This time it's different for you too. Each principle will build upon the next. If you follow this book in order, YOU CAN NOT FAIL!

I suppose you could always quit, but I don't BELIEVE that's the kind of person you are!

So where to start?

EVERYONE should start on page one and walk through the book in order.

Advanced/intermediate players may go through some beginning chapters more quickly. However, don't let your ego move you too quickly. There's a wealth of information in this book. Just because you understand part of the principle does NOT mean you have mastered everything about those principles.

The mind that is open to learning will become greater. The mind that thinks it knows everything already *will not grow*! It will only be a rock star in its own mind... Even <u>advanced players</u> will learn from these core chapters.

Take your time with each chapter. If you start getting frustrated, make sure you're not expecting too much of yourself before giving adequate practice to the specific task you're having an issue with. HAVE FUN!

Thank you for purchasing my book. I really appreciate it! Please Rate and Review this book on Amazon. I appreciate everyone's feedback. Thank you so much!

Go to: www.yourguitarsage.com/book-review

If you enjoyed this book then please recommend it to your local library. Thank you!

Introduction

Congratulations for finding this book and THANK YOU for purchasing it! By purchasing this book, as well as my guitar resources at www.yourguitarsage.com and www.unstoppableguitarsystem.com, I am allowed to reach people all around the world...and for that I am very grateful!

Before we begin, I want to let you know a little about myself and my approach towards teaching guitar. I have been playing guitar for over 25 years and have been in numerous bands (rock, metal, country, pop, alternative) during that time. I have studied with many teachers and was a classical guitar major for 3 years before changing my major and graduating with a Music Business degree. I am a working studio guitarist as well as a guitar teacher, songwriter, producer and live performer.

I LOVE playing guitar as a "job" and I am *living my dream!* I also **LOVE** imparting others with knowledge so that they, too, can fulfill their dreams as it relates to the guitar. I originally set out to teach a lot of people all over the world with a method that was fun, painless and to the point. I have taught guitar since I was about 17.

First, I just taught my friends and eventually 100s of guitarists professionally. I moved to Nashville, TN in 1990 and immediately hit the ground running. My clientele consists of students from ALL age groups and all walks of life including students, professionals, writers, producers, artists and record companies.

Since I have always been so obsessed with the guitar, teaching sometimes up to 65 students a week was not enough! SO, I started teaching for free on YouTube. Last I checked in the summer of 2013, my YourGuitarSage YouTube channel at www.youtube.com/yourguitarsage has over 30 million views and over 112 thousand subscribers.

On that channel I have taught hundreds of songs and techniques in MANY genres of music. I have received thousands of letters/e-mails from countries saying that they don't have the resources or money to take one-on-one lessons and that the only way they've learned how to play guitar was through me, Erich Andreas, AKA "YourGuitarSage".

Make sure you check out the Resources Page of this book to get a TON more free goodies and resources to keep you rocking on the guitar.

SOOO...Thank you for allowing me to guide YOU in this great learning process. I am thankful for this great opportunity!

A word of encouragement - Some of the concepts that you are about to learn are quite "thick" with information; you **WILL** be challenged to do some serious thinking about the guitar. Your hands will be as equally challenged. Many guitar players can mimic other players, but often times they don't know the "whys" of what they are doing or even how to be creative themselves.

This guide will unravel much of that. Your fingers will be more challenged than ever before. Your mind will be stretched much further as well. There is a reason why babies drink milk from birth, yet as they grow older, start eating solid food. This learning process is the same and it is crucial that you keep that in mind.

Before embarking on this journey, you must remember that you **WILL** get discouraged at times! You **WILL** get frustrated – and most likely, you will want your skills to progress faster...and to that I say, **WELCOME TO THE CLUB!** Most every musician wants things to move faster than they typically do. The greatest guitarists have *ALL* felt these frustrations and have also felt, at times, that they were not "cut out" for guitar. But like all good, worthy endeavors, we must strive for the mark.

If gold were just a few inches beneath the soil in our own backyard, we would be digging it up all day and probably wouldn't appreciate it much at all. But because it's found deeper – and requires considerable effort to extract it – it's much more valuable and appreciated *that much more*!

So be encouraged!

Remember that the time you spend on the guitar *WILL* pay off! Have *FUN* and spend as much time as you can playing, practicing and honing your skills. I promise you *WILL* see *great progress*!!

NOW DIG IN!

Chapter 1: How to Choose a Guitar for Purchase

Choosing a guitar is an exciting, but sometimes confusing undertaking because of all the variables that you might feel are involved.

What brand is best?

What type of woods?

Should I get an electric or acoustic?

What style...size...string-type...color and then what about all the things you don't know about guitars, right?

Let's simplify the process a bit.

Firstly, you probably have an idea whether you want an electric or acoustic guitar. Acoustic guitars are those guitars (typically with a sound hole) that are loud enough to be heard without amplification. Sure you can hear an electric when not plugged in, but it sounds pretty wimpy without an amp.

To seemingly complicate the matter, we have acoustics that can be plugged in for amplification, making them electric, and there are semi-hollow electric guitars, making them "acoustic" to a degree. The style of music and how you will be playing will often times be the determining factor as to what type of guitar you will want to get. Usually the heavier the music, the more an electric will suit you.

There are not a lot of "Screamo" bands playing acoustically these days and not a ton of bluegrass players shredding a Les Paul through a Marshall stack.

With that being said, the rules have been broken so there is nothing holding you back from doing either of those or anywhere in between. Let's talk a bit about the differences between the two before going any further.

Acoustic guitars don't need an amp, so they are nice and portable. The action (distance from string to fret board) tends to be a little higher than electrics and the strings are typically thicker, making bending and intricate licks/noodling *more difficult*. They sound great playing open chords and fingerpicking.

On the other hand, electrics usually have

lower action making soloing and subtle movements easier. I'm asked a lot about what beginners should start with. For different reasons I would choose both, but most of the time, I would say an acoustic would be my choice. There is less to be distracted by with an acoustic and you can play so many different styles easily on the acoustic. When directing a student to a new guitar purchase, the main variables for me always come down to: *budget, feel* and *sound* (in no particular order).

Trying a bunch of guitars in your price range will give you a great education on feel and sound. I KNOW you want the pretty red guitar, but don't pick the guitar because it's red if it sounds or plays poorly. The prettiness will get old. Poor sound or feel does not go away.

If you have a $300 budget, there is no need in seriously looking at the $1000 guitars, although knowing what they feel and sound like would be helpful to your education. I have some expensive guitars and some "cheapos." Sometimes more money gets you "more guitar" and sometimes more money just makes you think you are getting a better guitar.

I recently played two different classical (nylon string) guitars. One was $5000 and the other was $100. Can you guess which one sounded and played better? You would be surprised.

For one, I was not in the mood to drop $5000 on a classical, so that price range was not a consideration. However, if I did not look at the prices or brands, the $100 guitar played and sounded as good as the $5000 model. ***Now, this does not always happen, but it happens***. There are some great cheap guitars and some terrible expensive ones. Higher prices usually equate to better woods, craftsmanship, etc., but manufacturers are getting really good at producing good guitars at cheaper prices.

DON'T let the price alone dictate a guitar purchase. You will be sorry. So, figure out what your budget is and try to stick to it. You can get an acceptable $150 acoustic or electric if you know what to look for. I have guitars priced from $100 to several thousand dollars, but none were purchased regarding price alone.

Let me clarify: more expensive guitars TYPICALLY equate to better guitars, but be careful in using price to determine a guitars worth.

Feel is an important variable in

choosing an instrument. In fact, there are so many other variables other than the guitar itself that dictate sound (strings, pick, technique, etc.), whereas feel is a harder thing to change on a guitar. For smaller folks and kids, there are ¾ and ½ size guitars that might be easier to play chords on. There are different full-sized acoustic bodies like jumbo, dreadnought and parlor as well. But you don't need to know the names.

Use your common sense. If a guitar body is too big, try a smaller one. Electric bodies usually run much smaller than acoustics.

String action is also important as high action (string height) can make chording and fretting difficult and discouraging. The only way for you to know what is "normal" or "high" is to try a bunch of guitars. Try some expensive ones too, so you can get an idea for different price ranges and what the extra money may or may not buy you.

Keep in mind that string action can usually be adjusted, if everything else works for you. Many electric guitars have adjustable bridges. Acoustic guitar bridges can be "shimmed" or trimmed to give optimal action. Most guitar necks are also adjustable.

However, neither of these adjustments are ones that I would suggest beginners to attempt. I prefer to have an expert adjust them, however with experience and trial/error you can get pretty good at this type of thing. Okay, so all that said, make sure the "feel" of the guitar is the best out of all the guitars that you try.

Sound is the other important variable. Different woods and their ages, string types, pick type etc., are some of the variables that dictate sound of the guitar. Make sure that you are comparing apples to apples, such as comparing guitars with the same pick, playing the same songs, etc.

Even playing in different rooms will make the guitar sound differently. If playing several electrics, make sure you are playing them all through the same amp with the same settings. A bad sounding guitar through a great amp will typically sound better than a great guitar through a bad amp, so USE THE SAME VARIABLES!

Buying a first guitar is best done at a store where you can get an education in the process. <u>Don't be afraid to ask questions</u>, try a bunch of guitars and get what you want. Be polite, but you are getting ready to spend some money, so don't be rushed or talked into something that does not resonate with you (feel, sound and budget). It's okay to consider other prices and find out about different woods, etc. but ultimately it's what YOU are most happy with, not the sales person.

Take brand names with a grain of salt. There is not a best guitar, <u>only what's best for you</u>. There may be more suitable guitars for specific jobs, but keep an open mind. That is, don't buy a guitar just because of the name. I have brand name guitars that you would know and others that you would not, but I love them all for different reasons.

BUDGET, FEEL and SOUND... repeat the mantra after me... BUDGET, FEEL and SOUND... BUDGET, FEEL and SOUND. Now go fall in love with a guitar!

Chapter 2: Anatomy of the Guitar

As with learning anything new, it's very important to become familiar with nomenclature. I've provided this graphic so you can learn and can get used to using the proper terms for the components of your guitar. You'll just sound smarter, too!

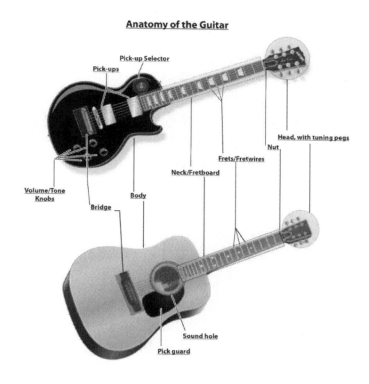

Anatomy of the Guitar

Chapter 3: Proper Posture

This is the first guitar lesson that I teach every new student.

No matter the style of playing, <u>EVERY</u> student must understand a few basic principle techniques that they will use for the rest of their guitar playing. THIS is the guitar lesson that covers them!

I'm going to break this down into some basic bite-sized pieces:

Posture - Make sure that your guitar is supported by your guitar strap. Don't have it so low that you can't play your chords correctly. No amount of "cool look" replaces bad playing. If you are not using a guitar strap, make sure that your guitar is supported by your legs, arm/body etc. so that you are NOT holding the guitar in place with your fretting hand. That type of grip will only ensure that you won't be able to play chords/scales well.

Hold the guitar pick comfortably, but

firmly between the index finger and thumb.

Hint: If you are doing a lot of heavy acoustic-type strumming, check out some thinner picks, instead of medium and heavy gauge. They will tend to pull out of your hand when strumming the guitar, if they are too thick. Also, if you do go with a thin pick, get "nylon" type guitar picks as they tend not to split like standard picks do. Save the medium and heavy gauge picks for more intricate electric or acoustic playing. I use all different gauges depending on what I'm playing. My rule is: the more intricate the picking the heavier the gauge and vice-versa.

FINGERTIPS!!! This is **THE #1 rule for ALL beginner guitar players**. For the fretting-hand, play on your fingertips! Playing on the "pads" of your fingers is bad practice and will make for sloppy playing and all sorts of frustration later down the road.

A good rule of thumb to remember is: ALWAYS keep your top knuckle of the fretting-hand curved. The only exception to this is if you are doing bar chords or double-stops (more on that later).

Chapter 4: How to Play Guitar Tablature – Part 1

Guitar tablature is a system of notation that graphically represents music by showing you the strings and frets that are to be played. It also can show some degree of "feel" or technique with slides, hammer-ons, pull-offs, slurs, vibrato, etc.

Since tablature is somewhat of a shortcut system there are not a lot of official rules to this notation. In fact, transcriptions vary from tab to tab as one transcriber may illustrate something differently than another.

That being said, I'm going to try to be as thorough as possible regarding the subject so that you have a good grasp of how to interpret it.

One thing that tablature does not illustrate is the duration of notes. It does not tell you how long a note should be held out. Sometimes tab transcribers will specifically put longer spaces between notes on the line to denote duration, but it's not quantifiable; it is simply a basic idea.

That being said, most people don't use tablature unless it's a song that they already know and can hum, so that part becomes less of an issue, except with more intricate parts.

Also, even though tablature has been around for centuries, some of the techniques used by rock/pop guitar players are <u>fairly new</u>.

<u>In tablature, each line represents a string on the guitar</u>. The thickest string is the bottom line and the thinnest string is the top line. So basically, it's the opposite of the way that you think it might be. One way to remember this is to think of the **higher lines as the higher pitched strings and the lower lines as the lower pitched strings.**

```
1st  string or e  ─────────────────────────── thin string
2nd string or B  ───────────────────────────
3rd  string or G  ───────────────────────────
4th  string or D  ───────────────────────────
5th  string or A  ───────────────────────────
6th  string or E  ─────────────────────────── thick string
```

The numbers placed on those lines represent the frets, NOT which finger is used.

Tablature does NOT tell you what fingers to use. That is where a good guitar instructor or proper technique comes in handy!

When numbers are placed vertically like below, you will play them like a chord (all at once), as in a strum.

Below is a G major chord.

```
1st  string or e  ——3——————————————————————————  thin string
2nd string or B  ——3——————————————————————————
3rd  string or G  ——0——————————————————————————
4th  string or D  ——0——————————————————————————
5th  string or A  ——2——————————————————————————
6th  string or E  ——3——————————————————————————  thick string
```

Part 2 of this section can be found later in the book. For now, you will only need to understand the principles in Part 1.

Chapter 5: Dexterity

"Getting your fingers to do what you want them to do..."

According to Webster's dictionary, dexterity is, "<u>the readiness and grace in physical activity; especially the skill and ease in using the hands</u>". Well that obviously applies to us guitar players; the more you do a particular exercise or movement, the better you become.

In fact, our brains are designed in such a way that it's impossible for you to not get better when you practice. That means that any amount of playing on the guitar whatsoever is beneficial. Now when we practice specifically, deliberately and with repetition, we end up gaining a lot of control over our fingers - or anything else that we set our mind to, for that matter.

Since our thumb is located so closely to our first and second fingers, our third and fourth fingers don't get called on for the same amount of tasks throughout the day.

For this reason, <u>EVERYONE'S</u> third and fourth fingers tend to be lazy when playing guitar. You thought it was just you? Nope! Hendrix, Van Halen, Vai and any other player that you can think of, had to develop their third and fourth fingers with exercises, many times, these exact same exercises. The only guitar players that don't have this issue are those that are born with a thumb that grows straight from the middle of their hand. :)

Yes, I'm toying with you!! Everyone has this issue, *so let's find out how to undo it!*

The following three exercises were specifically designed to strengthen your fingers and hands, increase your speed and sharpen your technique. I have used these exercises for years and have found them to be extremely beneficial.

Exercise one is a warm-up just to get your fingers moving.

Exercise two is an intense workout that develops both left and right hands. You will especially feel the third and fourth finger of your fretting hand being worked out through this one. Make sure that you're using the appropriate finger on the appropriate fret throughout the exercise. For instance, when you start playing frets two and three, make sure you are using fingers two and three. When you're playing frets three and four, make sure you are playing with fingers three and four.

Exercise three is a unique exercise that will seriously challenge you and require you to play on your fingertips. Don't be concerned if you can't do this exercise right away. It's definitely one you want to work up to doing. This third exercise can be fingerpicked or sweep picked. If you are going to use a guitar pick to do the sweep pick, pick the first three notes down and the second three notes up. Also make sure that when you do pick each string, it's done in a sweeping motion - NOT picking each note individually. It should be a smooth motion, allowing the pick to do the work. If you still have questions after reading this, please see the associated videos.

At the bottom of these dexterity exercises, you will see I also cover four things that you always want to remember when playing these exercises. Let me give you a little bit of theory as to why we are doing each of these things.

1. Playing on your fingertips makes a guitar player faster and more

efficient. The more you play on your fingertips the lighter your touch will be and the less hand fatigue you will experience. It's very important to also have control over what part of the finger you use. Since the fingertips seem to be the hardest part to master, learning this first will make everything else seem easier. Guitar players that play on their fingertips tend to play chords cleanly. Guitar players that play on the pads of their fingers tend to play chords sloppily.

2. **Playing right behind the fret requires much less pressure than playing further back.** Think about the leverage of a seesaw. The position of the fulcrum - that part under the center of the seesaw that balances it – determines how much leverage you have. On a see-saw, if the fulcrum is in the correct place, a small child can easily lift a large man off the ground. Similarly, leveraging your finger closer to the fret will allow you to play more quickly and efficiently.

3. **Playing with all your fingers is very important because, as you become a more accomplished guitar player, you will most likely be playing faster**

and/or more complex arrangements. Running out of fingers is no fun! So be proactive and use that third and fourth finger. I have had many students over the years thank me for insisting that they use their third and fourth fingers.

4. **Lastly, it's helpful to leave some space between the palm of your fretting hand and the guitar neck because it allows you to more easily play on your fingertips and ultimately have more control of your hand.** At first, this can be a little awkward. Most beginners grab the guitar neck like a shovel and their thumb comes right over the neck. And that's perfect... if you are digging a hole with your guitar! But you're not...so don't!

What we do on the guitar requires a lot more finesse and a much different approach than digging a hole. If we have a guitar strap holding up our guitar or if our guitar is being cradled by our legs and/or arms, then the guitar is not going anywhere. Once you are truly aware of this, it will liberate your hand from grappling the neck.

For new guitar players, grappling the neck can really limit your playing. Later on in your playing you may be able to be more carefree, but for now try to stick to good technique.

I am often times asked, *"How long should I practice this exercise?"* To which, I pose this question, *"how good do you want to get?"* Obviously, the more you practice these exercises, the better you'll become. If you want to become fast, you should practice it a lot. If you are perfectly fine with mediocrity, then you don't have to play as much. Alright, enough talk! Off you go!!!

- Play directly on your fingertips - make sure nails on "fret" hand are always trimmed.

- Play right behind the fret (this is for leverage). Remember the see-saw example.

- Play with ALL your fingers (each finger plays a specific fret)

- It is best to leave some space between the palm of your hand and the guitar neck. This will give you much needed leverage to play on your fingertips. Curling the last knuckle on your fingers is also helpful.

Dexterity exercise #1 is a GREAT exercise for beginners to advanced players. You can practice it for long periods of time and is great for general agility and strength.

Exercise 1

Dexterity exercise #2 is designed for intermediate to advanced players and is a great agility and strength builder. You will especially feel a "burn" when using fingers 3 and 4. This will quickly get your 3rd and 4th finger to be as nimble as fingers 1 and 2.

Exercise 2

Dexterity exercise #3 is for ADVANCED players! It is a MAJOR strength builder and perfect for building chordal dexterity, stretch (reach) and strength. Take your time moving into this exercise. It's very challenging!

Exercise 3

Depending on where you are at in your playing, these different exercises will serve you in various ways. The more you do them, the more dexterous you will become. Bottom-line, more practice = better player, 100% of the time.

Alternate Picking Exercises using Exercise 1

Exercise 1

For some extra-special-bonus-points type practice, try using the following variations on the "1,2,3,4" picking exercise (use alternate - down/up - picking)

1234	2134	3124	4123
1243	2143	3142	4132
1324	2314	3214	4213
1342	2341	3241	4231
1423	2413	3412	4312
1432	2431	3421	4321

Chapter 6: How to Tune Your Guitar

Guitar Strings and Tuning Your Guitar

Bottom or Low E string

High or Top E string

6/E 5/A 4/D 3/G 2/B 1/e

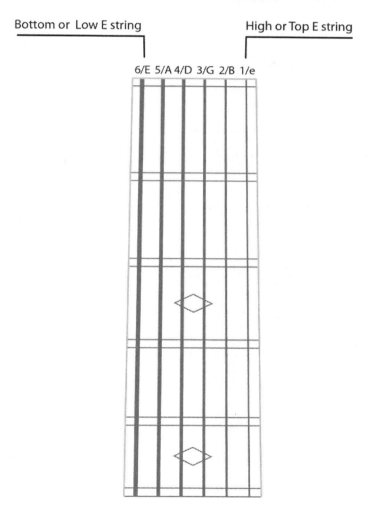

The thinnest guitar string is called the high or top string because it is the highest sounding string even though it is physically lower when the guitar is being held. It has a higher pitch than the other strings, which is why it is called the high E. Conversely, the thickest string is the low string because it has the lowest sound.

You MUST learn the names of your guitar strings if you want to take the guitar to the next level. From the thickest to the thinnest it is: E (6th string), A (5th string), D (4th string), G (3rd string), B (2nd string), E (1st string). You'll need to know this to properly use a guitar tuner or keyboard to tune your guitar.

An easy way to remember the names of the strings from low to high is:

E*ddie*

A*te*

D*ynamite*

G*ood*

B*ye*

E*ddie*

Silly, I know! But you won't forget it!

When a guitar string is out of pitch, it will either be sharp (#), or flat (b). If a string is flat, then it's lower than our desired pitch and would need to be tightened in order to sharpen the pitch. If a string is sharp, then it's higher than our desired pitch and would need to be loosened in order to flatten the pitch.

So when you turn your tuning pegs and the pitch lowers, you are flattening the pitch of the string. When you turn your tuning pegs and the pitch raises, you are sharpening the pitch of the string.

If you need a guitar tuner then you can use this guitar tuner video to help you tune your guitar.

Go to: www.yourguitarsage.com/guitar-tuner-video

Tuning Your Guitar to Piano or Keyboard

For those of you who play a little bit of piano.

1. Find middle "C" on the piano

2. Go 1 octave lower than that "C" and play the "A", two white keys to the left.

3. Strike the "A" on the piano and hold down the sustain pedal while you hit your "A" string.

4. To play the low "E", play the "E" that's 3 white keys to the left.

5. For the remaining strings D, G, B and E, find the notes according to the diagram below.

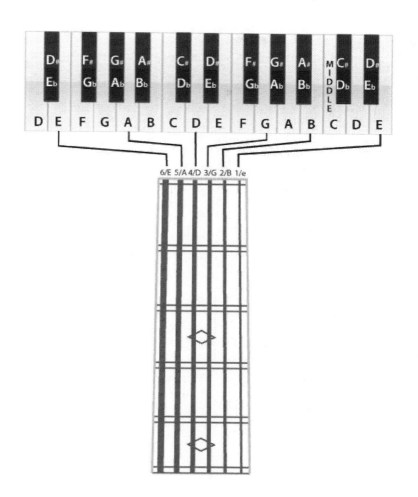

33

Chapter 7: How to Read Chord Stamps

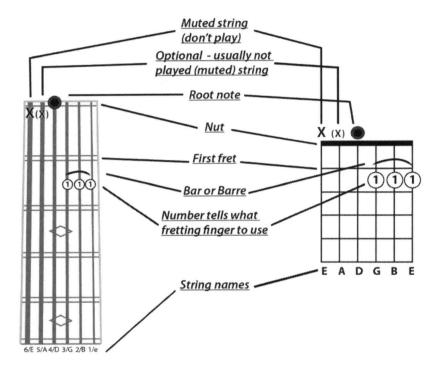

The above diagram is called a **Chord Stamp**. It allows us to easily read chord shapes. Many chord stamp illustrations vary, but for our example, let's go over the following:

The circle dot represents the root of the chord; the note that we build the chord upon. Essentially, it's the note that the rest of the chord is based on (i.e. "D", "D-", "D7" chords would all have different "fingerings", but would all have the same root, D). Often times, the root is the lowest sounding note in the chord.

The number within the <u>black</u> circle represents the fretting hand finger that should be pressed down on that particular place on the neck. "O" means open, or play that string without a finger on it. Sometimes I will put a "T" if I want you to bring your thumb up and over the back of the neck to play certain notes. However, you should not attempt that technique for quite some time as you will need to understand the "proper" way of playing chords before you try this "rogue" method.

Your fingers are notated:

Index=1, Middle=2, Ring=3, Pinky=4. The semi-circle/arc located above the three 1's on the chord represents a bar. A bar is when you lay your finger across several strings – like a bar. This can be tricky in the beginning, but don't over-think the process! Typically, a new player will only be able to bar 2 or 3 notes at a time. As your hand gets stronger and your technique increases, you will be able to bar all 6 strings when necessary! Don't worry about this now however. More on this later.

The "X" means *"don't play that string"*, or *"mute that string"*. It should not vibrate or make any sound when you play the chord. The "(X)" means that you can play the note, but for practical purposes, you usually would not. Technically, this particular note could be played in the chord without any "dissonance" (disagreeable notes/sound). If you do choose to play it, the chord will still sound "harmonic" (agreeable notes/sound).

Chapter 8: How to Play Open Chords

Playing open chords can seem like a daunting task for new players, but remember EVERY player goes through this. SO HANG ON!

First of all, remember the importance of playing on your fingertips. If you play on the pads of your fingers, you will NOT be able to play chords well! Observe your hand when you are playing. If something does not sound right, it's PROBABLY NOT! Play with the specified fingers to start off.

If you want to change fingerings after you have mastered these chords, then great! But for now, <u>stick to the specified fingering and you will quickly see your discipline pay off</u>. Arpeggiate (pick slowly) through the chord so that you can hear each note as it is being played. You will only cheat yourself by being sloppy, so pay close attention to your fingerings and technique.

When transitioning from one chord to the next, be aware of your fingers; which ones need to move where and what fingers stay in place,

(i.e. the 3rd finger never moves when going from a D to a G chord, or from a G to a D. For E to A-, all the fingers move together.)

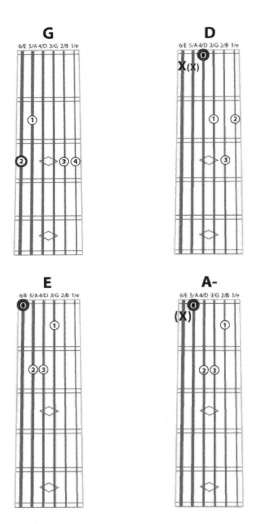

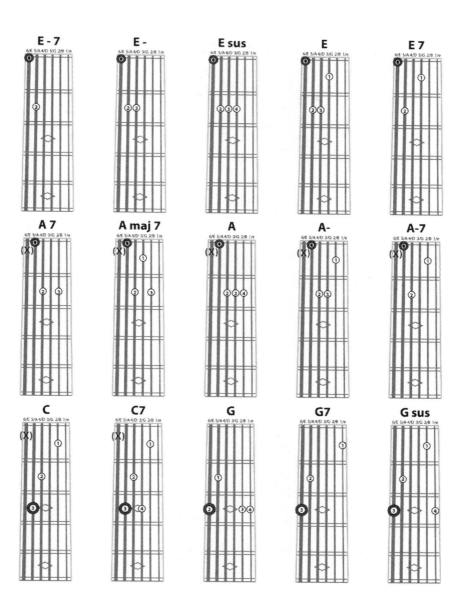

39

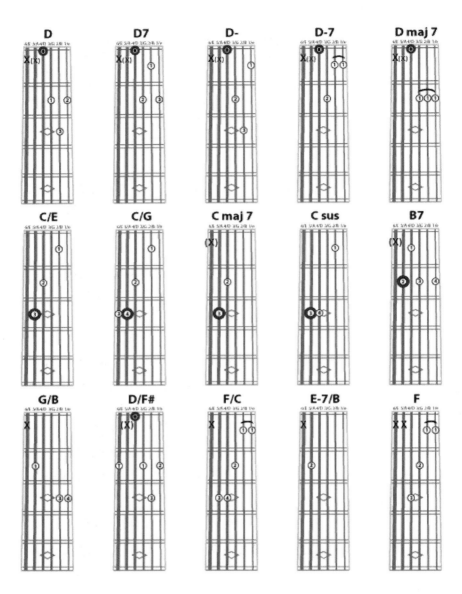

Chapter 9: Talent vs. Practice

Have you ever seen your favorite guitarist tear up a fret board without even seemingly trying?

Do you think they got that way because they were lucky, or because they were born into it?

Let me both disappoint and liberate you at the same time with the answer. **One guitar player isn't any luckier than another or born into playing licks easier than another.** If you were to take the top guitar players of each genre and find out how much they have practiced and how much they continually practice, it would be quite mind boggling. Is it a coincidence that only the great players are the ones that practice so much?

Obviously, you can see where I'm headed with this. Guitar players who have been playing for a long time and still have not progressed past a certain point, have not done so because of lack of talent; they've not done so because of their lack of practice!

If it makes you feel better to believe that Eddie Van Halen or any of the other great guitar players were born with a gift that you were not born with, then believe away only to the detriment of your own playing.

However, it's NOT the truth and that type of small thinking will hinder your playing exponentially. Don't believe the lie!

This is a subject that is rarely addressed or, often times, misunderstood completely. The definition of "talent" is a <u>natural aptitude or skill</u>. As far as practice goes, we all know what practice is and that doing more of it makes us better at whatever skill we are trying to improve. I know I'm going to step on some toes with this portion of the book, but bear with me because <u>I promise you</u> that what I am going to share with you in this section will only empower you to become the best player that <u>you</u> allow yourself to be.

Simply put, the point of this section is that the belief that you must be born talented or have some natural inclination to excel above the herd is not only completely false, but also extremely limiting to your playing... and your life!

Many people believe so fervently in this idea of an innate need for talent – as opposed to sheer practice – that they talk themselves right out of excellence! Defenders of the talent theory like to use examples of great icons that excel in a particular field or genre and say "there, you can't tell me that they are not talented!" They *assume* that the person was simply born with the ability they are displaying in their excellent performance.

This assumption, however, is very insulting and negates the thousands – or even tens of thousands of hours – that a person has spent "perfecting" their craft.

What do Jimi Hendrix, Amadeus Mozart, Michael Jordan and Thomas Edison all have in common? Well, depending on who you ask, some might say they were gifted or talented. Others, who have taken the time to step back, will realize that their gains are because of dedication, innovation, organization and perseverance. They understand that **the more one practices, the better one gets.**

Now I know that concept sounds logical, but see if you can step outside yourself for a moment and watch yourself slip into the "talent camp" when something appears to be out of your reach.

What I'm saying is, and I know this from personal experience because I used to do it often. It's easy to look at someone who has **"mastered his craft"** and say that they have some leg up on you. I've done it so many countless times throughout my life. I used to do it most often with musicians, but my love of illusions (magic), martial arts, etc., have also made me assume that somebody had a hidden key that I was not able to find.

I have played guitar for several decades now, have learned thousands of songs and have attempted to imitate hundreds of guitar players. I have seen success in all of these areas. I've had many people comment on how "talented" I am. The funny thing is, when I started playing guitar, I was *TERRIBLE!* Why is that?

It is that way because everybody is terrible when they just pick up the guitar! It's just that some folks forgot the process and how long it actually took them. Jimi Hendrix was terrible when he first picked up the guitar! Eric Clapton was terrible when he first picked up the guitar! Yngwie Malmsteen was terrible when he first picked up the guitar!

44

Are you getting the picture?

We would be much better off to replace the word talent with perseverance. Now that is a pill I can swallow! If someone said to me "the reason that a particular player does not play as well as Jimi Hendrix is because he doesn't have the talent," I would <u>never</u> concur. If someone said to me, "the reason that someone does not play as well as Jimi Hendrix is because they don't have the same perseverance that he had," I would wholeheartedly agree!

Perhaps to define it better, instead of the word perseverance we could even replace it with "efficient practice time." Now how unromantic is that? I know, it kind of makes you want to call it "talent" again right? How much cooler to think that we would not have to work and that we could just be born into such a thing. Let's not fall into the trap. It's lame and it's lazy and it's <u>NOT the truth</u>.

Jimi Hendrix started playing guitar somewhere around 10 years old. If he were so "talented", he would not have had to practice so much? Why didn't we hear of him breaking into the music scene at 10 or 11? What about Amadeus Mozart, Michael Jordan and Thomas Edison? Mozart was known to utterly surround himself with music. He was constantly immersed in it from a very young age. It's true that some people catch "the music bug" earlier than others, giving them several years more practice than others. That is a truism that you can't escape.

If someone starts playing guitar at age 4 as opposed to age 14, when both reach the age of 15 the one guitarist will have been practicing for 11 years while the other will have been practicing for one year. It's simple math. Can you see which player might sound better? Is this what we're calling talented?

I heard a story about Michael Jordan where he did not make the high school basketball team because he SUCKED! YES, that Michael Jordan!

However he was <u>determined</u> to play basketball. So he got that basketball out and started shooting hoops and still sucked for a bit, until continuous suckyness turned into kind of sucking, which turned into not so sucky, which turned into kind of good which turned into pretty good which turned into the best NBA basketball player to ever grace the courts!

Have you got it yet? It DOES NOT happen

overnight! He made his own destiny by being determined and practicing. In essence he became talented.

What about Thomas Edison? Who the heck is that you ask? He's the guy that invented the light bulb. Yep, pretty important huh? He also invented hundreds of other things that we use today. Look him up on Google if you want to see a man who has changed the lives of billions of people.

When Thomas Edison was creating the light bulb he used hundreds of different filaments before finding the right one. The filament of the light bulb is that little thing in the middle that glows. He used everything under the sun including horsehair but to no avail. <u>Finally</u> he got it right. Enter sarcastic Sage voice, "Boy, that talented Thomas Edison. He is just so lucky. Stuff just comes to him SOOO easily." Can you see how insulting that is when he worked his hind end off to create such a technology?

In fact, it was Thomas Edison who said, "genius is 1% inspiration and 99% perspiration" or in my words 1% talent and 99% practice. So that little 1% seed that was dropped into Jimi Hendrix, Amadeus Mozart, Michael Jordan,

Thomas Edison and YOU, must be watered and fed and given all the conditions to make that seed grow into fruition. That's the harder part. Seeds like that are dropped all day long but rarely do they find fertile ground. If you've gotten this far in my diatribe, I would guess YOU are fertile ground and are going to run with this information.

There is NO-thing stopping YOU from becoming the next Jimi Hendrix or Eddie Van Halen IF you practice like they did. THAT'S the tricky part. You were already born into this world with the ability!

Now that you know this, I want you to be aware of how you view great accomplishments. It does take a little bit of the wonderment away, but empowers you to create that wonderment for yourself. There is no task too great, or goal too lofty that you cannot attain if properly mapped out and walked through step-by-step.

This is not a pep talk, as I rarely have time for pep talks. This is a truism and is good news for those of us who are willing to work hard and smart. It's *bad news* for those that are waiting for talent or the Publisher's Clearinghouse sweepstakes guy with a big check to knock on their front door. Now, DON'T go easy on yourself. Go practice as if you are the next Jimi Hendrix, because you ARE!

Chapter 10: How to Master Strumming Quickly and Easily

Strumming the guitar can be frustrating if you are not shown the proper way to think and if you don't allow yourself some time to master some basic guitar rhythm skills. Here are some fundamental concepts that I want you to think about when practicing strumming.

1. Mute the guitar strings with your fretting hand (if you are a "righty," this would be your left hand). This will allow you to focus all of your attention on your strum.

2. *For the following exercises*, the numbers will **ALWAYS** be "down strums" (strumming towards the floor), while the "+" symbol (also known as the "and" of the beat) will **ALWAYS** be an "up strum." This is the KEY to good strumming. Be diligent with this basic principle.

3. Each strum should be equal distance from the last. If you are counting 1 + 2 + 3 + 4 +, the count should be smooth and even like a watch or clock ticking (unless you are "swinging the beat," which is not recommended before learning a basic straight strum).

4. Say the rhythm out loud, slowly. Once you get the idea, try to say that same rhythm in a seam less "loop" (meaning, don't stop at the end of the 4+). Once you get the hang of this, it should stream together like 1 + 2 + 3 + 4 + 1 + 2 + 3 + 4 + 1 + 2 + 3 + 4 +

5. Once you can count it smoothly like this, strum it slowly and steadily. If you are new to strumming, try the very first strum, which is 4 down strums on the down beats.

6. When the strum calls for a space or void like 1 + 2 + 3 + 4 or 1 + 2 + 3 4+, your hand should STILL move as if it were going to hit the strings. This way your down strums will always be where your down beats are and your up strums will be where your up beats are. Get it?

NOW for the exercises! For this study,
take it slow and go through ALL levels in order.

Level 1

1		2		3		4	
1	+	2	+	3	+	4	+
1	+	2	+	3	+	4	
1	+	2	+	3		4	+
1	+	2		3	+	4	+
1		2	+	3	+	4	+

Level 2

1	+	2		3	+	4	
1		2		3	+	4	+
1	+	2	+	3		4	
1		2	+	3	+	4	
1	+	2		3		4	+
1		2	+	3		4	+

Level 3

1	+	2	+	3	+			+
1	+	2	+		+	4	+	
1	+		+	3	+	4	+	
	+	2	+	3	+	4	+	

Level 4

1	+	2	+			+		+	
1	+		+			+	4	+	
	+		+	3	+	4	+		
1	+		+	3	+		+		
	+	2	+			+	4	+	

Level 5

1		2	+		+		+
1	+		+		+		+
	+		+		+		+
1		2	+	3			+
1		2	+		+	4	+

If you find that you are having trouble with a rhythm or two, check out this video which will teach you a couple of ninja guitar tricks and will help you through the rough patches and allow you to master any rhythm. Master ANY Guitar Strumming Rhythm With This Secret Technique go here: **www.yourguitarsage.com/master-guitar-strumming**

Remember to TAKE IT SLOW and don't get the fretting hand involved until you feel consistent about the strumming hand. With diligent time and practice you will get REALLY good at this.

Are you enjoying the material that is in this book?

If so, the next time you are at your computer can you leave me your feedback?

It's super easy and I really appreciate you!

Go to www.yourguitarsage.com/book-review

Thanks in advance!

Chapter 11: How to Read Chord Charts

Learning to read chord charts is **fun and easy**. It will open a new world of songs to you, as you will now be able to unlock the "code". I use charts all the time in the studio, live and as a teacher, especially for songs that I am not familiar with, or don't have the time and need for memorizing. This method of playing music is not too dissimilar to preparing a speech and then reading it, or referring to your notes throughout the speech. Most bands that play together a lot don't use charts because they have played the songs enough times to have them memorized.

There are many chart types, but only a few that you see often. The type that we will be covering today, is the most common and most useful. The charts we will be covering are standard and "number" charts. There are several things that need to be covered before we can unlock these charts.

Meter – Most songs begin and end with

the same "meter". Meter is defined as: rhythm that continuously repeats a single basic pattern. About 99% of today's music is in "4", which means that the basic pattern repeats every four beats. Most other tunes are in 8 or 6, where the pattern repeats every 8 or 6 beats respectively.

Every now and then, you will find a song written in an "odd" time signature like 5 or 7. "Money" by Pink Floyd is in 7. If our chart says, "In 4," that means that pattern for the most part will repeat every four beats. If there is a strumming rhythm, it will typically repeat every four beats as well. If you have trouble counting to the music, here are some things that will help you.

1. Most songs emphasize the "1" beat. It's when most chords transition from one to another.

2. The snare drum (the very loud beat that you can hear easily on recordings) is usually the "2" and "4." The snare drum is that high pitched, loud drum that sits between the drummers knees. It sounds a bit like a clap.

Feel and Capo – If the song needs a capo, it will typically be denoted like "Capo 3," etc. This would mean that you would put the capo at the 3rd fret. Using a capo, "transposes" the actual chords. Often times, charts won't mention the feel of the song. (feel = what key the song feels like, for example – C or G major) That's no problem though. Just capo where requested and act as if the capo is the "nut" of the guitar.

If you move the capo to the 3rd fret, you will need to play your chords 3 frets higher than you would if you did not use a capo. I will often denote the feel of the song, especially if it's a "number" chart. This way you know what chord to play for the number represented. More on that later!

Groupings – Chords will be separated from each other when they represent a "measure." If a song is "In 4," you will see a chord separated by a space, and then another chord, etc. For a song like "Big Cheater", illustrated at the end of this chapter, each chord represents 4 beats. So there would be a total of 16 beats for the following chord progression (E-D C B7). If a measure has more than one chord in it, it's called a split measure and is denoted, by an underline.

For example, in the song "Hurry",

illustrated at the end of this chapter, the 10th measure of the verse is split, C D. Since this is still a measure of "4," "C" would get two beats and "D" would get two beats. In "Counting Song", illustrated at the end of this chapter, the intro and verses are all split. Since that song is in 4, each chord would get two beats because they share the measure. Then in the chorus it would be back to our normal full measure of four beats per chord. Sometimes you will see "hash" marks over the chords if it's not an evenly split measure.

In "Hurts", illustrated at the end of this chapter, you will find an "uneven" measure, in the 1st bar (measure) of the bridge. The "C" chord would normally be held out for 3 beats, and the "D" for one beat, but we have yet another notation to consider. The "p" above the "D," means that you "push" the D chord. Basically, you just play it a little earlier than you would normally play it. To be exact, you play the "D" on the "and of 3" not on the 4. If we count 1+2+3+4+, the C is held for 1+2+3, and the D is played on the + of the 3 and held out for +4+. This last part is a bit complex, so if you don't get it right now, don't worry.

Come back to it though, because even though you won't run into it very often, you will hear a difference.

Inversions – Inversions are chords that have another note from that chord that is played in the bass, instead of the "root." A "C" chord has a C in the root. A "D" chord has a D in the root, etc. Sometimes you will see a chord symbol like "C/E" as we see in the 3rd measure of the chorus of "Ellen", illustrated at the end of this chapter. Simply put, this is a C chord with an "E" in the bass. Normally when we play a C chord, we mute the low E string (6th or thick string) with our thumb, or we don't strum it at all. That would produce a sonically correct "C." However, when a "/" chord is represented, that usually means that another instrument (usually the bass) is playing that low note, instead of the root of the chord (i.e. "C").

Other examples that you will see often times are G/B, which means a G chord, with a B in the bass (2nd fret/fifth string). C/G is C chord with a G in the bass (3 fret/6th string). D/F# is a D chord with an F# in the bass (2nd fret, 6th string). I like to reach my thumb over the top of the neck and play that F# with my thumb (difficult for smaller hands). Often times you will have to change your fingering in order to produce this new inversion. If you don't quite get this section on inversions at first, don't worry. Learning is a process. Come back to it and eventually, it will make sense.

Also, whenever you see a "/" chord, you can safely play the chord to the left of the slash. If it's a C/E, you just play the C. If it's a D/F#, you can just play the D. If you are playing with a bassist, he would usually play the lower notes and your ear won't be searching for it. If you are playing by yourself (solo guitar), you might find something "missing" with the chord if you don't include that lower note.

Number charts – Often times, studio musicians (especially in Nashville) will prefer a "number chart". These charts refer to numbers instead of letters. The reason that studio players like these types of charts is that they are easy to transpose (change keys). Refer to the "number system matrix chart" for these examples. For "Hurry", the 1 represents the G and the 6 represents an E. However, there is a minus (-) after the E. That means that you make the E, an E- chord, instead of an E. The fifth measure of the verse is a 4, which in the key of G is a C chord.

The sixth measure is a 5, which in the key of G is a D chord. If we were in the studio and the singer wanted to try this in the key of C, instead of G, we wouldn't have to rewrite our charts. We would just have to "rethink" in the key or feel of C. In this scenario, the 1 would be a C, the 6- would be an A-, the 4 would be an F and the 5 would be a G. Another reason that we might want to change keys (other than the singer), is playing ease. This song is easier played with a G feel, so that our 5 chord is a D instead of an F (in the key of C).

However, in the 14th measure of the 1st verse, we find a 3-. In C, that would be an E-, which is an easy chord to play. In G, the 3- would be a B-, which is a bar chord and a more difficult chord to play. Using the capo helps us to limit bar chords, but sometimes they are unavoidable. Everything else however is consistent between number charts and standard charts. In a nutshell, number charts substitute numbers instead of letters.

Symbols and Notation – Since charts are condensed versions of actual music, there is often much left to the imagination. We can't hear a piece of music. It is lifeless, until a musician brings it to life! Symbols and notation help musicians get a better idea of what the composer or arranger wants, like road signs when we drive.

Since these are fairly impromptu and different from each chart writer to the next, sometimes you just have to use common sense. (i.e. if a chorus is followed by 3x, it typically signifies that you should play the chorus three times). However, you will see these symbols "[:" and ":]" or something similar fairly often. These denote a repeated section of music. If you were to see, "[: E- C G D:]," you would play E-, C, G and D and then repeat it. If the ":]" were followed by a 3x you would play for a total of three times.

In summary, charts will allow you to play music that you have never played before. At first your reading will be slower, just like it was when you first learned to read a book. Then as the months and years progressed, so did your reading. Sooner than later, you will be able to look at a chart and play it correctly for the first time, just like reading a book.

Remember... **PRACTICE, PRACTICE, PRACTICE!** ...and *HAVE FUN!*

Counting Song

IN 4 Capo 2 (C feel)

INT:	C G/B	A- F		C G/B	A- F

VRS:	C G/B	A- F		C G/B	A- F
	C D-	A- F		C D-	A- F

CHR:	G	F		G	F

VRS:	C G/B	A- F		C G/B	A- F
	C D-	A- F		C D-	A- F

CHR:	G	F		G	F

VRS:	C G/B	A- F		C G/B	A- F
	C D-	A- F		C D-	A- F

64

Big Cheater

IN 4 Capo (G feel)

INT:	E-	D	C	D
	E-	D	C	B$_7$
VRS:	E-	D	C	B$_7$
	E-	D	C	B$_7$
	E-	D	C	B$_7$
	A-	A-	B$_7$	B$_7$
CHR:	C	E-	C	E-
	C	E-	B$_7$	B$_7$
	C	E-	C	E-
	C	B$_7$		

TA:	E-	D	C	B$_7$

VRS: AGAIN

CHR: AGAIN

BRG:	E-	E-	G	D
	C	C	A-	A-
	B$_7$	B$_7$		
TA:	E-	D	C	B$_7$
	E-	D	C	B$_7$

CHR: AGAIN

65

Big Cheater (Number System)

IN 4 Capo 2 (G feel)

INT:	6-	5	4	5
	6-	5	4	3₇
VRS:	6-	5	4	3₇
	6-	5	4	3₇
	6-	5	4	3₇
	2-	2-	3₇	3₇
CHR:	4	6-	4	6-
	4	6-	3₇	3₇
	4	6-	4	6-
	4	3₇		
TA:	6-	5	4	3₇

VRS: AGAIN

CHR: AGAIN

BRG:	6-	6-	1	5
	4	4	2-	2-
	3₇	3₇		
TA:	6-	5	4	3₇
	6-	5	4	3₇

CHR: AGAIN

Hurry

IN 6 Capo 5 (G feel)

INT:	G	E-	G	E-

VRS:	G	E-	G	E-
	C	D	G	D
	G	<u>C D</u>	E-	C
	D	B-	E-	E-

CHR:	C	C	E-	E-
	C	C	G	D
	G	D		

Verse and chorus 3x total , then

VRS:	G	E-	G	E-
	C	D	G	D
	G	<u>C D</u>	E-	C
	D	B-	E-	E-

CHR4:	C	C	E-	E-
	C	C	G	D
	C	C	E-	E-
	C	C	G	D
	G			

Hurry (Number System)

IN 6 Capo 5 (G feel)

INT:	1	6-	1	6-

VRS:	1	6-	1	6-
	4	5	1	5
	1	<u>4 5</u>	6-	4
	5	3-	6-	6-

CHR:	4	4	6-	6-
	4	4	1	5
	1	5		

Verse and chorus 2x, then

VRS:	1	6-	1	6-
	4	5	1	5
	1	<u>4 5</u>	6-	4
	5	3-	6-	6-

CHR4:	4	4	6-	6-
	4	4	1	5
	4	4	6-	6-
	4	4	1	5
	1			

Ellen

IN 4

INT:	[:C	C	E-	E-:]

VRS:	E-	E-	E-	C
	<u>C E-</u>	E-	E-	E-
	C	<u>C E-</u>		

CHR:	[:E-7	E-6	C/E	E-:]

VRS:	E-	E-	E-	C
	<u>C E-</u>	E-	E-	E-
	C	<u>C E-</u>		

CHR:	[:E-7	E-6	C/E	E-:]

INT:	[:C	C	E-	E-:]

VRS:	E-	E-	E-	C
	<u>C E-</u>	E-	E-	E-
	C	<u>C E-</u>		

CHR:	[:E-7	E-6	C/E	E-:]

Hurts

IN 4 (Capo 1 G feel)

INT:	[:E-	D	C	C:]

VRS:	E-	D	C	C
	E-	D	C	C
	C	C D	E-	E- D
	C	C	C	D

CRS:	E-	E- D	C	C
	G	G	D	D
	E-	E- D	C	C
	G	G	DSUS	D

TA:	E-	D	C	C

Verse and Chorus again, Then bridge

	III p		
BRG:	C D	D	C	

SOLO:	E-	E- D	C	C D
	E-	D	C	C

CRS:	E-	E- D	C	C
	G	G	D	D
	E-	E- D	C	C
	G	G	DSUS	D
	C	C	DSUS	D

70

Chapter 12: Number System Chart

Major	1	2	3	4	5	6	7
Quality	Maj	Min	Min	Maj	Maj	Min	Dim
Key of A	A	B-	C#-	D	E	F#-	G#°
Key of B	B	C#-	D#-	E	F#	G#-	A#°
Key of C	C	D-	E-	F	G	A-	B°
Key of D	D	E-	F#-	G	A	B-	C#°
Key of E	E	F#-	G#-	A	B	C#-	D#°
Key of F	F	G-	A-	Bb	C	D-	E°
Key of G	G	A-	B-	C	D	E-	F#°

Major	1	2	3	4	5	6	7
Quality	Min	Dim	Maj	Min	Min	Maj	Maj
Key of A-	A-	B°	C	D-	E-	F	G
Key of B-	B-	C#°	D	E-	F#-	G	A
Key of C-	C-	D°	Eb	F-	G-	Ab	Bb
Key of D-	D-	E°	F	G-	A-	Bb	C
Key of E-	E-	F#°	G	A-	B-	C	D
Key of F-	F-	G°	Ab	Bb-	C-	Db	Eb
Key of G-	G-	A°	Bb	C-	D-	Eb	F

71

Chapter 13: How to Practice to Chord Charts

If you are still new to chords and moving between them, it's best to 1st practice your transitions. To do this, move your fretting hand (relax the strum hand) back and forth between two chords. Just toggle <u>back and forth</u> without strumming, being mindful and exact about your fingering. **Try this for a bit with all the chord transitions in a song.** Once you get the left hand "working," you can strum to make sure the chords sound nicely.

Remember that every great guitar player struggled with the same chords that you and I struggle with. <u>DON'T GIVE UP</u>!! Just be observant of your hands when you hear something that's not right. Once you have the transitions down, it's best to play the chord on the "1" and hold it out for the full measure or four beats (if the song is in 4). Often times this is called a "diamond." You will see this written in many of my charts when a chord is to be held out for a full measure.

Playing in "diamonds" will get your internal metronome (clock) in better sync with the music. Once you get the "feel" of diamonds, you can start strumming on each single beat. If you know what the strumming rhythm of the song is, you could then practice that, but not before getting the "diamonds" and single note strums down. Here is the breakdown for practicing these charts:

- **Transitions**

- **Diamonds**

- **Single Beat Strums**

- **Actual strumming rhythm of the song**

Chapter 14: How to Use a Capo

    A capo (pronounced "cape-o") is a moveable bar that can be attached to the fingerboard of a fretted instrument to uniformly raise the pitch of all the strings. Capos allow us to play songs in different keys, without altering our fingering.

    Remember, the musical alphabet is as follows: *A, A#, B, C, C#, D, D#, E, F, F#, G, G#*

    Let's say we have a song that is in *G* (Major) and the chords are *G, C, A-* and *D*. If we want to transpose (change keys) that song up a half step (1 fret), then we would place the capo at the 1st fret and move our chords up 1 fret as well. Doing this allows us to play in our new key of *G#*, while still allowing us to play in a "feel" of *G*. If we did *NOT* use the capo, we would have to play four bar chords (*G#, C#, A#-* and *D#*) - which is *no fun!*

    With our capo at the 1st fret, we will have transposed to *G#* without having to play all those pesky bar chords! This will also allow us to free up some fingers to add ornamental parts to a once basic chord progression.

When I chart a song, I will notate at the top of the page if you need a capo and where you should put it on the neck/fret board. I will also sometimes denote what "feel" the song will be in. For the song example in the above paragraph, I would notate "Capo 1(G feel)".

G, C and *D* are the easier keys ("feels") to play songs in. You will often find songs that are in another key, but you can simply use a capo and follow the chord structures of those easier keys.

It's easy to transpose using the number system chart that I have created; if you can work a little basic math, you don't even need it, though. If you use the musical alphabet above, you could capo 1(*G* feel) to play in *G#*. To play in *A* with a "*G* feel", capo at the 2nd fret. To play in *B*, with a *G* feel, capo at the 4th fret. Similarly, you can do this for keys *C* and *D*. If you want to play in the key of *D*, but with a "*C* feel", capo at the 2nd fret.

no capo/ open	C	G	D	A	E
1	C#	G#	D#	A#	F
2	D	A	E	B	F#
3	D#	A#	F	C	G
4	E	B	F#	C#	G#
5	F	C	G	D	A
6	F#	C#	G#	D#	A#
7	G	D	A	E	B
8	G#	D#	A#	F	C
9	A	E	B	F#	C#

Capo on Fret Number

So what type of capo should you buy? *My* favorite brands are *Kyser*, *Shubb* and *G7th*. The Kyser is a very easy to use clamp style of capo. It's also handy because you can easily clamp it to the head stock of your guitar when you're not using it - so you'll always have it when you need it! While I like using the Kyser for the quick "on and off" needed during live acoustic gigs, I have found that it seems to throw my electrics out of tune a bit from the pressure of the spring.

For this reason, I prefer the adjustable style of the Shubb and G7th for when I'm playing live with an electric (if I desire a capo) and for studio work with both acoustics and electrics.

Chapter 15: Fingerpicking

Fingerpicking is the use of one's fingers to strike or pluck the strings instead of using a pick (plectrum). This technique is widely used in classical, flamenco, Spanish and folk music; however, it has also been used in nearly every genre of music - including pop and rock. Fingerpicking allows the player to be more selective regarding what strings should sound when playing the guitar polyphonically (multiple simultaneous notes).

For example, if I want to play an E minor chord, but don't want the fourth and fifth strings to sound, I would either need to mute them or just not play them at all. If I were strumming the guitar, you can see how playing the same chord without the fourth and fifth strings might be awkward.

However, with the use of fingerpicking I can pick strings 1, 2, 3 and 6 easily. That's a very simple explanation of the myriad of possibilities that only fingerpicking will allow. Fingerpicking also has its own distinctive sound.

When reading music that uses fingerpicking, you may see the term "PIMA" or the initials P, I, M or A used. PIMA is an acrostic for the thumb and the first three fingers of the right hand. Because of its length, the pinky is often times not used. PIMA is often utilized to indicate which fingers to use in picking. The traditional Spanish words that we derive those letters from are:

Pulgar = Thumb

Indice = Fore Finger

Medio = Middle Finger

Anular = Ring Finger

I know! I don't speak Spanish either. It's certainly a lovely language, but we need something else to help us remember the fingers. Here's how to think about them.

For P, think of the guitar pick - or if you're in the UK, they call it a plectrum. A lot of beginning guitar players will use their thumb instead of a pick. Got it?

- For I, think of the index finger

- For M, think of the middle finger

- For A, think of the anniversary (ring) finger

Fingerpicking, like any other technique that we are going to study, requires practice, attention and a lot of patience. This is a technique that feels awkward at first and too, with time and discipline, miraculously gets easier. If the definition of an arpeggio is a broken chord or a chord where the notes are played independently of each other, then you are about to play a lot of arpeggios.

Until you get more comfortable with the fingerpicking hand playing the prescribed patterns, it's extremely important that you focus all of your attention on the fingerpicking and not the fretting. For this exact reason, I want you to start this process by playing an open E minor chord, on strings 1, 2, 3 and 6 only. We won't be playing strings 4 and 5, which are the only strings that you would be fretting for our traditional E minor chord.

So, let your fretting hand relax. You won't be using it to start off here. Now with your fingerpicking hand, place your thumb (P) on the sixth string, your ring finger (A) on the first string, your middle finger (M) on the second string and your first finger (I) on the third string.

Now, just rest your fingers there for a moment. I want you to indelibly (forever etched in your mind) picture how your fingers are sitting on the strings. Remember this one concept and fingerpicking will almost never be an issue for you. How your fingers are sitting on the strings is the basis of 99% of the fingerpicking that you will encounter. Don't take your fingers off the strings just yet!!!!

Now, notice the two headings on the fingerpicking exercise page follow this description: "Songs in 4" and "Songs in 6".

The first example under "Songs in 4" says PIMA. That means if the song count is 1, 2, 3, 4, you would pick P, I, M, A, or thumb, index, middle, ring. You get it? I knew you would... you're smart like that. Once you get this basic feel down, work your way down the list. This may take 5 minutes or it may take an hour. There is no crime in over practicing. It will only make you more ninja-like!

So the next exercise would be P, I, A, M, and so on. Practice each exercise for a few minutes. This will assure that you have a good feel before moving to the next exercise. When you're done with that list, move over to the next list to the right, where you will find finger combinations. When you see two finger letters underneath a beat, that means that both of those fingers should be played simultaneously (at the same time). On the 3rd list to the right we have more of the same, only this time the thumb shares in the combination pick. This is what is referred to as a pinch-pick. It is called a <u>pinch-pick</u> because the motion looks much like a pinch if executed properly.

When you come to this list, this section will make more sense.

Fingerpicking can be done in any time signature. *However*, 4/4 and 6/8 are by far the most common. In fact, they will make up the majority of the songs that you encounter. To get you started, I have included 28 exercise patterns. Granted, some of these patterns you will never use, but many of them you will.

As an exceptional guitarist, however, we want to be versatile! Practicing **all the patterns** will not only develop your dexterity in regards to fingerpicking, but it will also get you to start "thinking outside of the box" and coming up with your own patterns. Depending on the genre of music, picking with your nails is preferred over not having nails and playing with your fingertips.

Classical, Spanish and flamenco styles almost always require the use of fingernails while country "chicken pickin'" sounds better when you don't have nails. YOU are the artist here. You get to choose what best suits you. Be open and experiment with some different styles to see what you're most comfortable with.

Fingerpicking Exercises - Songs in 4

1	2	3	4
P	I	M	A
P	I	A	M
P	M	I	A
P	M	A	I
P	A	M	I
P	A	I	M

1	2	3	4
P	M A	P	M A
P	I M	P	I M
P	I A	P	I A
P	M A	P	I M
P	I M	P	M A
P	I M A	P	I M A

1	2	3	4
P A	M	I	M
P I	M	A	M
P M	I	A	I
P M	I	P A	I
P A	I	P M	I
P I	M	I	A

Fingerpicking Exercises - Songs in 6

1	2	3	4	5	6
P	I	M	A	M	I
P	M	I	A	M	I
P	M	A	M	I	M
P	I	A	M	A	M
P	M	A	M	I	M
P	A	M	I	M	I
P	A	I	M	I	M

1	2	3	4	5	6
P	I M A	I M A	P	I M A	I M A
P	I M	I M	P	M A	M A
P	I A	I A	P	I M	I M

Chapter 16: Where the Notes Fall on the Fret Board

The "line" notes (*EGBDF*) appear on the musical staff as shown below:

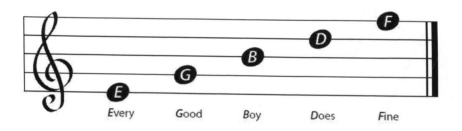

The "space" notes (*FACE*) look like this on the musical staff...

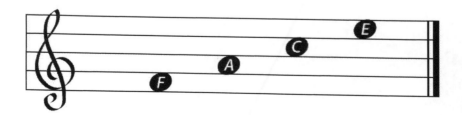

From the low open *E* string to the fifth fret
of the high *E* string, here's what it looks like...

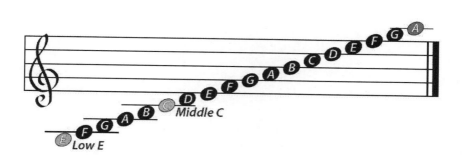

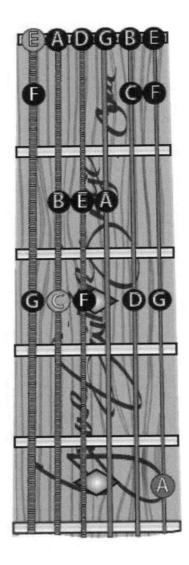

Now, when you locate these notes on the fret board of your guitar, you find the Low E (the lowest note on your guitar with standard tuning); middle C and the high A from the above staff - *all within the first 5 frets!*

Chapter 17: Springboards

I'm often asked by students, *"How can I find my way around the fret board more quickly?"*

When watching a great guitarist, they often times make it look effortless or even impossible. Without knowing the tricks it seems like magic. But alas, it's knowledge and VERY attainable. Let me emphasize that these are learned skills. Sometimes I'm also asked why one would even care to know the notes on the fret board.

Some players may never desire to know such things, or what they play does not require them to know it as readily. But what they don't know CAN hinder their playing.

Don't misunderstand what I'm trying to convey. You might go your whole life and play in a band and NOT know the notes on the fret board. However, in certain (and many) settings, if you don't have that knowledge, you are going to look pretty silly NOT being able to play something that is required of you.

Let's say, I walk into a studio and the producer hands me a chart that is in the key of C - I sure better know where a C is! If I don't, I'm going to have problems playing a solo or improvising in any way. So the short of it is, knowledge is power and since you are smart enough to be filling your head by reading this, I trust you are someone that wants to excel and are ready for the challenge.

When it comes to knowing your fret board, there are a myriad of techniques that you can use to determine which note they are playing at any given point in a song. Below are two diagrams I refer to as "springboards", which are great tools to enable you to know exactly where you are on the fret board.

Stationary Springboards Diagram

1. Know the names of your open strings E, A, D, G, B and E. Also, remember where your root notes are for all your open chords - E, A, D, C, G etc.

2. Know the octaves of your open strings which are at the 12th fret and those open

chord roots which are exactly 12 frets higher than their originals. So there your E, A, D, G, B & E are again.

3. Remember how we learned to tune the guitar to itself using that 5th/4th fret technique? Well, since you know that already you have another springboard.

4. 12 frets up from the notes found on that tuning technique will give you yet another springboard location.

Movable Springboards Diagram

All the numbered dots on the diagram below are "C" notes.

1. *Notice numbers 1 and 5. They are strings E and A. ANY note on those strings will have an octave available down 2 strings and UP 2 frets as denoted by numbers 2*

*and 6. So 2 goes with 1 and 6 goes with 5.
Get it?*

2. *Now notice numbers 2 and 6. These are
on strings D and G. ANY note on those
strings will have an octave available
down 2 strings and up 3 frets as denoted
by numbers 3 and 7. So 3 goes with 2 and
7 goes with 6. See, now you are getting it!*

3. *Now check out numbers 3 and 5. I use
this one a lot, too. Since these are both on
E strings (high and low), they will always
be mirror images.*

4. *You could also associate, for instance, 1
and 4 or 5 and 2, etc., but the others are
more apparent. The more you know, the
better a guitarist/musician you become.*

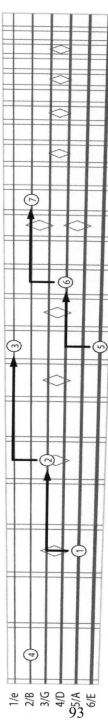

1/e
2/B
3/G
4/D
5/A
6/E

93

Chapter 18: Diatonic Harmony

- The musical alphabet goes from A to G (there is no "H, I, J", etc.)

- A half-step is the distance between 1 fret and the next on a guitar

- A whole step is equal to 2 half-steps or 2 frets distance

- A sharp (#) is when we raise a pitch by a half-step

- A flat (b) is when we lower a pitch by a half-step

- Every note has a sharp, except for **B** and **E**

So, the musical alphabet reads like this A, A#, B, C, C#, D, D#, E, F, F#, G, G#...

... and all the notes on a 23 fret board look like this (next page)

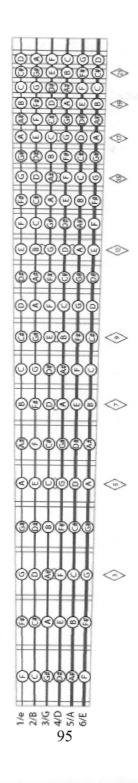

95

So, if W = whole step and H = half-step, then: Major Scale = W W H W W W H

Scale steps: 1 2 3 4 5 6 7 8 (or 1)

Distance between notes: W W H W
W W H

Have you ever heard the vocal exercise, "Do-Re-Mi-Fa-So-La-Ti-Do"? Those are the musical steps for the major scale. Or the "Do Re Mi" song Julie Andrews sings in "The Sound of Music?" That song is based on the steps of the major scale. It is VERY important to learn the major scale if you want a good foundation for learning everything else on the guitar. It is the basis of music theory, the field of study that deals with the mechanics of music and how music works.

Definitions To Know

Interval – The pitch distance between 2 notes.

Chords – 3 or more notes played together.

Arpeggio – "broken" chord, or notes from a chord played apart from each other.

Major Chord – 1st, 3rd and 5th scale steps (notes) from the Major scale: 1, 3, 5.

Minor Chord – 1st, flat 3rd and 5th scale steps (notes) from the Major scale: 1, b3, 5.

Chapter 19: The Major Scale

The major scale can be defined as a 7 note scale separated by the following intervocalic distances: whole-step, whole-step, half-step, whole-step, whole-step, whole-step, half-step (W W H W W W H). The major scale is **the most important scale** that we will address. It's the benchmark scale that we compare all other scales and chords to. When you hear a musician describing a scale or chord with terms like "flat three", "sharp seven" etc. they're referring to adjustments of the major scale to create this other scale or chord. "Trust me now, believe me later"... learn the construction of the major scale and know how to use it to create chords and scales as I have and will continue to show you through my lessons.

It is important to be able to construct major scales across a single string. It's important to see this pattern and to be able to recreate it on any string and from any fret. If you have not done so already, it would behoove you to master this lesson and get that skill down.

Knowing this construction is obviously crucial, but then we must graduate to more usable forms of the scale.

See the diagrams at the end of this chapter for the first form of the major scale that I want you to learn.

I use this form all the time to determine the key of a particular song, to construct chords, to analyze chords and a myriad of other musical reasons. Another great thing about this scale, as with all scales on the guitar, is that it is completely mobile or movable. Unlike a lot of other instruments - like the piano or wind instruments - the guitar allows its player to transpose scales very easily by playing the same pattern lower or higher up on the fret board. That is to say that if you took the G major scale and move all the dots up one fret and play the same exact pattern one fret higher, you will now be playing the G#(sharp) major scale.

Move it up another fret and you will now be playing A major. Take that same G major scale and drop it down a half-step, or one fret towards the nut or tuning pegs and you will now be playing in the key of Gb(flat) or F#(sharp). For more advanced guitar players this concept is not new to you. For those that are just coming to understand these concepts it's important to understand how the scales move. It will **save you a ton of energy and time** if you grasp this concept correctly now instead of skipping over it.

So again, all the dots within a specific scale will move up uniformly. For instance if you're moving the scale up 5 frets, every dot moves up 5 frets exactly. You will use the exact same fingering higher up the neck that you use in lower positions near the nut. This is a skill that can be developed with perseverance and detail. *Don't be a slacker!* Learn this scale and open up your playing. As we progress in our studies I'm going to show you that this is the most useful tool for a guitar player to know.

Practice makes perfect, and allowing your fingers to practice what your head just learned is a surefire way to integrate this into your knowledge. So this is how I want you to practice the scale. Place your fretting hand in the 2nd position (this means to slide your hand up 1 fret from the open position so that your 1st finger is behind the 2nd fret, your 2nd finger is behind the 3rd fret and so on).

For this scale, keep your hand in this position. Don't move your hand up or down the guitar neck while you play the scale. Doing so will better ensure that you play the correct fingers on the correct fret. Now play through the scale slowly and systematically and say the scale step numbers for each note as you play it (for example 1, 2, 3, 4, 5, 6, 7, 8 (or 1)).

This will help with developing your ear and understanding the number system. This will also increase your finger dexterity and help to increase speed. Don't try to play the scales quickly, however. That will only slow your learning process. There is plenty of time, once you master the scales, to play them quickly.

Once you get G major down, slide the entire form up one fret. Remember that all the notes should move up 1 fret uniformly and that the fingering will be exactly the same as it just was for the G major scale. Before you play each scale, **audibly say the name of the scale** (for example, "G# major"). This will help you understand what you are playing. Continue to move the scale up the guitar fret board one fret at a time and naming the scale before you play it. Do this across the entire fret board until you get to the end.

Make sure that you play the same scale down the fret board towards the

nut. It may take a little figuring out – which is good for your brain - but attempt to play the scale in the open position as well.

Notice on the second diagram how we can play this same form starting at the 5th string instead of the 6th string. This will save you time by allowing you to memorize one form and use it by starting from either the 6th or 5th strings. To play the fifth string root form of this scale you will start in the same position (2nd) for C major. You will use the same exact fingering.

Also, *don't forget to audibly say the name of the scale as you play it.* The letter name of the scale is the first scale degree. Again, play this all the way up the fret board and play it down to the open position as well.

In regards to picking the scales, the beginner guitarist should probably stick with down strokes while the intermediate and advanced guitar players should incorporate alternate picking (strict up and down picking). Alternate picking can be frustrating and difficult in the beginning (and is for everybody who just first attempts it). So if you're attempting alternate picking, take it slowly.

The brain learns a lot faster when you do

things slowly. Trying to do this quickly when you haven't done it systematically and slowly will only slow down your learning process. Don't fall into the trap that says you have to practice fast to play fast.

Now stop reading, and go get that guitar!!!

In the following diagrams, the finger I want you to use to fret the indicated note is marked right under the fret board. The tonic (root) note of the scale is indicated by the dark circle around the note.

6th String Root G Major Scale Form (1 octave)

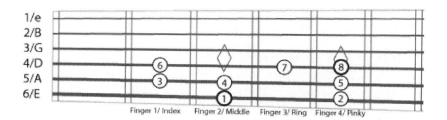

6th String Root G Major Scale Form (2 octave)

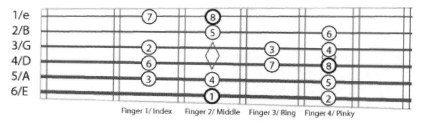

103

5th String Root C Major Scale Form (1 octave)

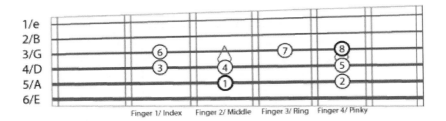

5th String Root C Major Scale Form (2 octave)

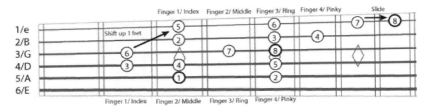

Single String Scale F Major Scale (1 octave)

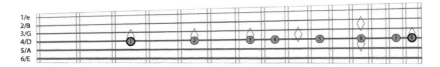

Thank you for all your support! Please leave your feedback by leaving your book review. Thanks in advance! Go visit:
www.yourguitarsage.com/book-review

Chapter 20: Relative Major and Minor

For every major key there is a relative minor key. Conversely, for every minor key there is a relative major key. In short, these relative keys share the same set of notes.

For example, the key of C major contains the following set of notes: C, D, E, F, G, A, B; while the key of A minor has the same set of notes: C, D, E, F, G, A, B. Because these scales share the same notes, they have a special relationship that we refer to as being "relative." Since "A" is the tonic or key in "A minor," we usually see the notes written in this order: A, B, C, D, E, F, G (as a side note, it's common practice to start and end scales with their tonic note). This works the same for all keys.

The key of G major contains the following set of notes: G, A, B, C, D, E, F#; while the key of E minor has the same set of notes: G, A, B, C, D, E, F# - making them relative as well. However, we would usually see the notes in the key of E minor written in this order: E, F#, G, A, B, C, D.

So why should we care about the subject of relative major and minor? Because it will literally double your productivity in regards to music theory, lead guitar and a myriad of other applications. <u>With this knowledge</u>, knowing one major scale would allow you to play over any major or minor chord progression! More on that later!

So make sure you read this entire section through several times until you get the concept. It's invaluable knowledge that will increase your understanding of the fret board and music in general.

Now let me show you the easiest way to find the relative major or minor of any song in any key. Here is the rule: If you know the major key that you are in, move down exactly one and a half steps, or 3 frets on the same string and that specific note's name will be the relative minor key.

For instance, let's say we are looking for the relative minor of G major. On the low E string, play the G on the third fret. Moving down three frets or one and a half steps from this fret will bring you to the open E. Remember how we said earlier that G major's relative minor was E minor?

Let's try another example with C major. So play C on the A string, which is the third fret. Moving down three frets or one and half steps from this fret will bring you to the open A. Remember how we said earlier that C major's relative minor was A minor?

I can feel you getting it!

Okay, let's try one last one for the key of D major. On the open A string play the D, which is the 5th fret. Now you try it yourself. What was the rule? Move down 3 frets or one and a half steps. You should have discovered the "B" at the 2nd fret. So B minor is the relative minor of D major. Conversely, if a song is in a minor key and you want to define the relative major, you just do the opposite by moving up 3 frets.

If you wanted to find the relative major of A minor, you would move up three frets from the open A, which would give you a "C". See how easy that is?

<u>So here's the fun part!</u> If you know any songs in a minor key, find out what the tonic is, move up 3 frets from the tonic and you have your relative major. Now you can play that major scale over the song in the minor key and it will sound harmonic or pleasant to your ear. It's

helpful to know all the major and minor scale forms. I will sometimes use this technique to play a scale that I'm less familiar with to see if it produces different melodies and licks that differ from what I might normally play.

So now you might be saying to yourself, *"Why even differentiate between a major key and its relative minor if they use the exact same notes?"* Think about the subject of a speech for a moment. If I said that I was doing a speech about war, it could be in support of war or against war – depending on how I phrase things. This speech on war might include keywords like: money, defense, lives, freedom, etc., but HOW I use these words determines my stance. <u>Get it?</u>

The relative major/minor relationship is very similar in that we are using the same notes (words and phrases of the speech), but we are saying it differently in each scenario and emphasizing different notes as per what key we are in. Also, think of the actual subject of the speech as the tonic. The <u>tonic of the key</u> is often times the note that is used to <u>end</u> a musical phrase. So if we were in the key of A minor, many of our phrases will end with an A, while in the key of C major many of our phrases would end with a C.

As you know by now, I am a big advocate of putting things learned into **practice immediately**. If these concepts make sense to you without picking up a guitar, then they might stick with you for a little while. However, putting them to practice immediately will make them a VERY real part of you – so don't sell yourself short!

Your homework is to find the key of any song. How do you do that? For a small amount of folks, you will be able to do this "by ear." For those that have not developed this technique yet (yes this is a LEARNED skill), find out the key to the song of your choice using any means available (ask a friend, do a Google search, watch a tutorial, grab the sheet music, JUST DO IT!!).

If a song is in a major key, find its relative minor using the above method. Or even better yet, if it's in a minor key, find its relative major and try your hand at "noodling" the major scale over the top of that song. To start off you may just play the scale up and down, but as that becomes boring to you, try to come up with your own phrases, licks or musical ideas. No matter how simple or silly you think they may sound, they are the workings of great masterpieces.

EVERY composer, rock star, and songwriter has started at these simple steps. They are CRUCIAL and you going through the exercises are going to make you the guitar player that you envision.

Now go pick up your guitar!!

Although you already know how to do this without the below cheat sheet, here's a list of each major scale and its relative minor.

C b major – A b minor

G b major – E b minor

D b major – B b minor

A b major – F minor

E b major – C minor

B b major – G minor

F major – D minor

C major – A minor

G major – E minor

D major – B minor

A major – F# minor

E major – C# minor

B major – G# minor

F# major – D# minor

C# major – A# minor

Chapter 21: The Power of the Pentatonic Scale

A pentatonic scale is a musical scale with 5 notes per octave - in contrast to a heptatonic (seven note) scale, such as the major and minor scales.

The pentatonic scale is easily the most widely used scale throughout world music including rock, pop, blues, jazz and other contemporary and traditional genres of music. It differs from the major scale in that there are 2 notes not present. Musicians evaluate chords and scales according to the major scale (It's our benchmark for comparing chord and scale embellishments). So, if you took the 4th and 7th note out of the major scale you would have the major pentatonic scale.

Yep, it's that simple!

But there is something special about the pentatonic scale that makes it sound unique and why it's so widely used. Think about the ingredients in a recipe. A simple recipe with 3 or 4 ingredients can often times taste better than something with 30 ingredients.

In the case of notes, more is not always better. If we are comparing the major pentatonic scale to the major scale, then the notes represented would be 1, 2, 3, 5 and 6. Remember we said that the 4th and 7th notes of the major scale are not played.

The minor pentatonic has the *same shape*, but as you will see in the diagram that follows, it would be played in a different place. If you already know the minor scale, then just take out the 2nd and 6th scale degrees (notes) - everything else stays the same. If this part does not make sense to you, hang in there. You can also learn this by memorizing and knowing how to use the forms.

So how would we actually use this scale? Play an A minor pentatonic scale over an A minor chord progression and it will sound pleasant to the ear. For instance, have a friend play the following progression: A-, C, F, G. Then play an A minor pentatonic scale over that and you will find that it is "harmonic," or pleasant to your ear (no bad notes). The G major pentatonic scale played over a G major chord progression will also sound harmonic to your ear. Have a friend play this progression: G, G, C,

D and play a G major pentatonic scale over that and you will find it pleasing to your ear.

Note that you must use the associated minor pentatonic scale over a minor chord progression (i.e. - A minor pentatonic over an A minor chord progression. Conversely, you must use the associated major pentatonic scale over a major chord progression. For instance, if my chord progression is in "A minor," then I would use the A minor pentatonic scale. If my chord progression was in "A major," then I would use the A major pentatonic scale over the top of it and it would sound harmonic.

These are good "rules of thumb" to follow; however, music is art and technically there are no rules in art! Anything goes! I say that for two reasons. The <u>first reason</u>, if you play music long enough, you will discover every rule being broken at some point. The second reason is to free your mind from rules that might limit you in music.

With that being preached, a good musical rule to live by is "Learn all the rules...and then forget them!" There have been many musical greats that have said similar things, so adhere to this wisdom.

For instance, in blues, it is common practice to play a minor pentatonic scale over a major chord progression. "But you just said..." I know! Musical rules can be broken, but not before you learn how to do it the "right" way first. Try it for yourself. Check out my lesson on the 12 bar blues progression. The chord progression that I cover is A7, D7 and E7. Those 3 chords are major chords. Visit: www.yourguitarsage.com/12-bar-blues

In fact, when played together, those 3 chords create a chord progression that suggests that A major is the key. However, the A minor pentatonic scale sounds great over this. Try it out for yourself with a friend. In fact, try both the A minor pentatonic scale and the A major pentatonic scale and see how differently each one sounds.

So what can you do now that you have this knowledge? Well, in short you can play melodies over nearly any chord progression that you hear. In order to do this, first find the song's key. Ask someone, look at the sheet music, Google search it, do SOMETHING. If it is in a major key, use the associated major pentatonic scale over the top and "noodle" around with the notes to create melodies.

A lot of Tom Petty's songs use the pentatonic scale, but again he doesn't make it a rule, it just happens a lot. Conversely, if the song is in a minor key, use the associated minor pentatonic scale to noodle over the top of it. Get it? If it's an A minor chord progression, then use an A minor pentatonic scale. If it's a G# major chord progression, use a G# major pentatonic scale. It's that easy!

Another great way to practice is to take some songs from your MP3 player that you already know, find out the key and noodle over the top of it. Also, it's helpful to play the song several times in a row while you do your noodling so that you can get the feel and tempo of the song. While you're doing this, notice how each note of the scale sounds. You might notice that one note wants to move to another note. This is called "tension." Notice how the tonic or root note sounds good at any time. It is the most restful note since it is the key of the song.

Also notice how any other note other than the root played at the end of a phrase makes the phrase sound like a question. That is to say that ending a phrase on the root note sounds like the period at the end of a sentence and any other note makes it sound like there's more left to be said - as if the note were a question mark or comma.

Once you get the hang of this, another exercise that I love to do is to put the radio on, use my ear to determine the key of a song, and then noodle over the top of it with the appropriate pentatonic scale. When the next song comes on, do the same thing. Some of you won't be able to do this as your ear hasn't developed yet, but it will in time. This exercise will develop both your ear and lead playing skills VERY rapidly.

The Pentatonic Diagrams and How to Practice Them

This is always where the rubber meets the road. ***Reading and doing*** are 2 different things and I promise you that the "doing" of this will most likely help you to understand this concept better than the reading portion. So, if the last few pages left you shaking your head in confusion, be encouraged because you are going to get ALL of this.

As I say to my students all the time, it's helpful to look at a particular concept from several different angles. Doing so allows you to understand it at a deeper level. This goes for all subjects in life, not just guitar or music.

Now take a look at the pentatonic diagrams on the following pages. I have separated these into the A minor pentatonic scale and the C major pentatonic scale. Also notice how both these scales share the same exact notes and the same exact patterns, but their tonics or key centers (the dark circled notes) are different.

Why is that?

Because C major's relative minor scale is A minor (that means that they share the same set of notes). So considering everything that I've discussed already about how to use what scales over what progressions, all of the A minor forms of the pentatonic scale would work best over an A minor chord progression. To use the C major pentatonic scale, it would sound best over a C major chord progression. Now I can already hear you asking, "But they are the same scale, why can't I use either?" The answer is you can. They are the same exact scale, however over the C major chord progression, "C" is your tonic or key; over the A minor chord progression, your tonic is "A."

Form 1 of these diagrams is by far the most important scale pattern in all guitar playing, in all of history, for all genres, Amen!

118

Let me say it again, form one is an invaluable pattern that you will find in all genres of guitar music. Learn it, memorize it and know it inside and out, backwards and forwards. After you have mastered form one it's up to you which forms you want to learn. I like to work my way out in either direction of form one.

Memorizing each of these forms may take you several weeks, or an hour of concentrated practicing. Once you have all the forms memorized and don't have to look at the diagrams any longer, start moving them up the fret board 1 fret at a time. At first you will probably only be comfortable with moving one pattern up the fret board until you reach the end of the neck. Make sure that you work it down the fret board and work it into the open position as well, not just down to the first fret position.

As you get more acquainted with each form across the entire fret board, then start thinking about using <u>all the forms in one particular key</u> before moving it up the fret board. Before you do this, it's a good practice to name the key that you are in. *For instance*, say "A minor pentatonic," before you begin the exercise and play through each form until you do a complete cycle of the guitar neck. I always start at form one and work my way up the neck.

119

When I run out of frets, I start over in the open position and continue on until I'm back where I started. Then I move to the next key, "A# minor pentatonic," and so on.

Once you do this for all the minor pentatonic scales in all the different keys, do the same routine for all the major pentatonic scales. Yes, I know it's the same forms, but starting the scale from the new major pentatonic key will help you to see these forms in both the major and minor relationship.

In regards to how to pick these scales, I practice them a few different ways. Depending on your proficiency, beginners should start off picking every note with a down stroke. After you have mastered all the forms and are then able to concentrate a bit more on the picking hand, it's important to start developing your alternate picking technique. To do this, pick the first note down and the second note up and follow this pattern to the end of the scale. Don't try to complicate this one. It's easy if you do it slowly! Just down, up, down, up, down, up, etc. Since this scale is so uniform and only has two notes per guitar string, it is a great exercise for practicing "hammer-ons" and "pull-offs".

Otherwise, pick the lower note on each

string and hammer the note just above it. If you want to practice your pull-offs, pick the higher note on each string and pull off to the note just below it. (See page 149 and 150 for examples)

There are literally months and possibly years of potential practice that can be gleaned from these exercises. I have used them for years and still do on a weekly basis. Be patient but persistent. These exercises will allow you to master your fret board and develop your left and right-hand techniques.

Here are the **Pentatonic Scale Diagrams.**

A Minor Pentatonic Scale

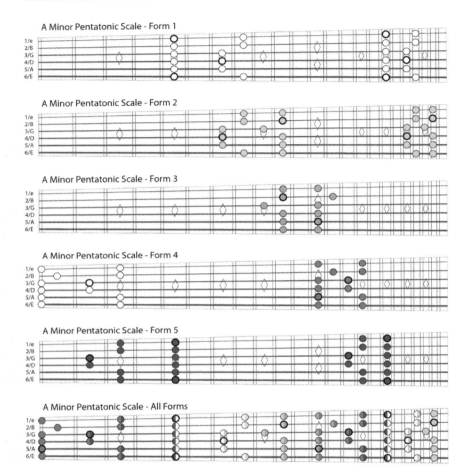

A Minor Pentatonic Scale - Form 1

A Minor Pentatonic Scale - Form 2

A Minor Pentatonic Scale - Form 3

A Minor Pentatonic Scale - Form 4

A Minor Pentatonic Scale - Form 5

A Minor Pentatonic Scale - All Forms

122

C Major Pentatonic Scale

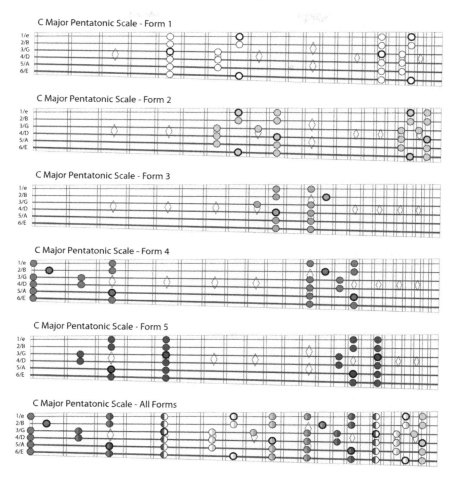

C Major Pentatonic Scale - Form 1

C Major Pentatonic Scale - Form 2

C Major Pentatonic Scale - Form 3

C Major Pentatonic Scale - Form 4

C Major Pentatonic Scale - Form 5

C Major Pentatonic Scale - All Forms

Do you need more help with learning the guitar?

Check out my free video course on how to quickly master both your fretting and strumming hand.

Visit www.unstoppableguitarsystem.com today.

Chapter 22: Chord Noodling Improvisation

Remember from our study of the major scale that for every key there is a certain set of notes that complement each other, as well as a certain set of chords? Have you ever wanted to know how a guitar player can play notes effortlessly all over the guitar neck and the notes that they choose, always sound good?   Have you ever noticed that your favorite guitar players don't just play "standard" chords, but in fact embellish and even play melodies over chord progressions, while they are holding chords?

I like to call this "chord noodling," meaning you are "noodling" around with different notes while still playing the chords. It's a SUPER cool way of making a standard chord progression sound PRO.

THAT is where the following fretboard noodling maps REALLY come in handy! Let's say you are playing a song in the key of G and the chords are G, C, E- and D. You could use the Chord Noodling Map in the key of G, to show you

EXACTLY all the safe notes that you could "noodle" with, while playing that chord progression.

So here is an exercise for you. If you know that a song is in one of the keys represented in the following maps, try to come up with an arrangement using some notes outside of the chord, but still in the key as represented by the map. If you DON'T know the key, use the Number System Chart in this book to identify what key the song is in by matching your chords with the appropriate key. For instance, if your progression is G, C, E- and D, then your song is most likely in the key of G and you would use the G map. If your chord progression is C, A-, F and G, then the song is most likely in the key of C and you would use the C map. Get it? Note: Don't get distracted by if the song needs a capo or not. If you are using a capo and playing the above chords, you will still use the corresponding map.

Check out these videos, if you still need help:
Guitar Chord Noodling Part 1:
www.yourguitarsage.com/chord-noodling-part-1

Guitar Chord Noodling Part 2:
www.yourguitarsage.com/chord-noodling-part-2

Chapter 23: Chord Noodling Maps in Open Major Keys

Key of A

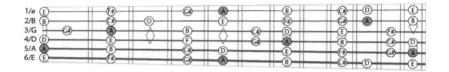

Key of C

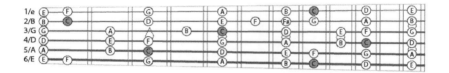

Key of D

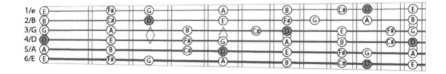

Key of E

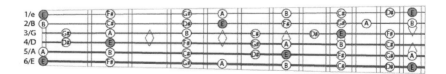

Key of G

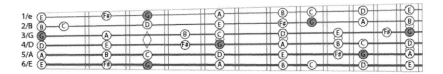

Chapter 24: Bar Chords

     Bar chords, also known as *barre chords*, are any chord that requires at least one finger to press down multiple strings simultaneously (at the same time). Bar chords allow guitarists to play chords that are not restricted to the open strings. Bar chords are known as movable chords as each form can be moved up and down the neck in a linear fashion. That is, one bar chord formation will allow the guitar player to play a chord in any key by merely moving it up or down the neck.

     Bar chords can be used **in conjunction with open chords or with other bar chords**. Bar chords are sometimes necessary when a song requires a chord to be played that cannot otherwise be played open. Any chord played in the open position can be replicated as a bar chord further up the neck, given of course that the guitarist has built the strength and dexterity to do so.

     "So hold on Erich! You are saying that *anything* I play in the open position can be played further up the neck in bar chord fashion to produce the same chord in every other key?" Yes! That one concept alone will open your playing up quite a bit. That means that many of those open chords that you know already are going to become our patterns or "templates" for the first set of bar chords that you should learn.

As you probably know already from watching my instructional videos on my YouTube channels, many of my lessons are based around open chords and the use of a capo. I try to keep things as simple as possible when teaching. My philosophy is, *"there's no need in complicating something that's not complicated."* There are plenty of intricate guitar parts that cannot be simplified. In those cases there is no way around it; however, sometimes even the simplest of songs call for bar chords and there's no way around that, either. The capo can be used to *limit bar chords* or change the forms of the open chords that you would use, but sometimes you just have to play a bar chord. In those cases wouldn't it be nice to have that ability?

Some guitar players might skip this section fearing the dreaded bar chords. While others may feel that their playing does not lack without bar chords. But that's not you! You want to excel as a guitarist and I am going to help you!

That being said, bar chords are challenging for guitarists who have never played them. Remember you *and your hands* are learning a new concept! Please be patient with yourself during this process and understand that everyone from Jimi Hendrix to Steve Vai had difficulty with bar chords in the beginning.

I have taught hundreds of students over several decades and have never met a student, even my best, who got this concept immediately. **So be encouraged**, take your time, watch the videos and enjoy the process. There are literally thousands of bar chords, but here we will only be using the ones that you will use the most. The more you practice them, the faster and better you will become.

I like to break the subject of bar chords down into two sections:

1. Understanding the forms

2. Playing the chords

Understanding the Forms

Check out the bar chord diagrams that follow the description below. You will notice that I have separated these as 6th string roots and 5th string roots in the bar chord diagrams later in this chapter. That means that the root or letter name of the chord is located on either the 6th or 5th string. For this first example see the 6th string bar chords page. Now locate the first major chord. Does anything look familiar about that form? That form comes from our open E major or E chord. Now look at the first minor chord form. Now play an E minor chord. Do you see the similarity? If not, hang with me! Now go to the bar chords page with the 5th string roots. Look at the first minor chord. This chord form comes from the A minor (A-) chord. Are you seeing the pattern? If not, check my videos on bar chords at:

Bar Chords Part 1:
www.yourguitarsage.com/bar-chords-part-1

Bar Chords Part 2:
www.yourguitarsage.com/bar-chords-part-2

Notice the dark circle that is in each bar chord. That circle represents the root of the chord. The root is essentially the one note that the rest of the chord is built upon. It is also the letter name of the chord. For instance, A major,

A minor, A7 and A-7 all have "A" as the root or letter name. The rest of the notes in the chord determine it's "flavor", as in: major, minor, 7, -7 etc. So that means every time you move that bar chord up and down the neck, the letter name of the chord changes also. Each of the bar chords on the bottom row of the 5th string roots page have the dark circle located at the 2nd fret of the 5th string which is a "B"; therefore, every chord in that bottom row has a "B" root. The "flavor" of the chord is located above the form. Therefore, if you moved each one of those chords up a half-step, you would then have a "C" in the root.

Get it? I knew you would!

Now that you understand where the forms come from and how they move about the fret board, let's talk about how to play them.

Playing the Chords

Understanding how the chords move about the fret board and actually playing the chords are two totally different things. When playing bar chords, lazy or poor technique will quickly limit you. There are a lot of other techniques - like playing single notes - which guitarists can "fudge," even with poor technique.

Not so much with bar chords... so trust me through this process. Watch the associated videos and **keep practicing** until you get this. <u>No one</u> gets this right off the bat; it is a learned technique that the more you do, the better you become. Now that we have that excuse out of the way, *let's do this thing!*

As someone new to playing bar chords, the following points are of utmost importance! If you find yourself having difficulty, make sure you are aware of the following:

1. The finger that does the barring MUST either be perfectly straight, or better yet hyper-extended. Here is a great exercise: Lift your fretting hand up and view your index finger from the side. While viewing it from the side, straighten the finger. Now go beyond that and see if you can't slightly bend the finger backwards. Obviously, our knuckles don't allow us to bend the finger back too far, but just that little bit is what we call hyper-extended. In this hyper-extended position, your finger is ideally situated for evenly distributing the weight of that finger across all the strings in your bar chord. Even if your finger is perfectly straight, this is a great place to start. I usually tell

my students to hyper-extend that finger a little bit because I know the natural tendency is to bend it the other way - which is awesome if you want your bar chords to sound like poo! If the barring finger is flexed or bent in its natural direction - even the slightest bit - during the bar chord, you *most likely* will have some unwanted muted notes.

2. In order to have that straight or hyper-extended barring finger, we need to make sure that our thumb is on the back of the neck closer towards the bottom part and not lazily hanging over the top of the neck. That may be fine for lead work and open chords from time to time, but it's the kiss of death when playing bar chords. ***So don't do it!***

3. Keeping your thumb on the back of the neck should allow for some space between the palm of your hand and bottom of the guitar neck. Again, at least in the beginning, you want to make sure that space is there, otherwise you will have difficulty with your bar chords.

4. For the fingers that are not barring, but are playing individual notes, make sure that those fingers are playing directly on the fingertips and not on the pads. *This is extremely important!* Seriously, for my students that are playing sloppy bar chords or claim that they can't play them at all, they are always breaking one of these rules... or several. "So listen to me now and believe me later." For those other fingers remember, "FINGERTIPS! FINGERTIPS! FINGERTIPS!"

For now, the trick will be to bar your barring finger properly, while properly playing on the fingertips of all the other fingers. If you don't give up and practice, *YOU WILL GET IT!!*

Practice, practice, practice!! You've heard me say it and you'll keep hearing me say it! You are only as good as how long and how well you are practicing! No one is a "natural" at this; anyone who desires this skill *must* practice it.

This kind of direction is difficult to put into words. You've heard it said before that a picture can say 1000 words. Well a video can

136

say about 10,000 words! Please watch the associated videos after reading this as they will clear so much up for you.

Bar Chords Part 1:
www.yourguitarsage.com/bar-chords-part-1

Bar Chords Part 2:
www.yourguitarsage.com/bar-chords-part-2

6th String Root Bar Chord Forms

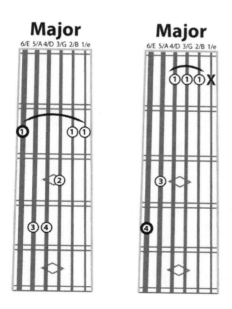

- or Min

6/E 5/A 4/D 3/G 2/B 1/e

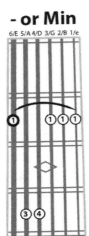

Sus or 4

6/E 5/A 4/D 3/G 2/B 1/e

11,4 or Sus

6/E 5/A 4/D 3/G 2/B 1/e

-7 or Min 7

6/E 5/A 4/D 3/G 2/B 1/e

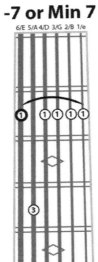

138

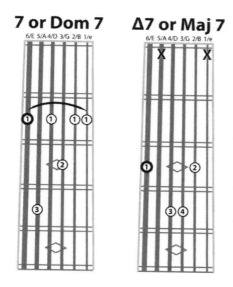

5th String Root Bar Chord Forms

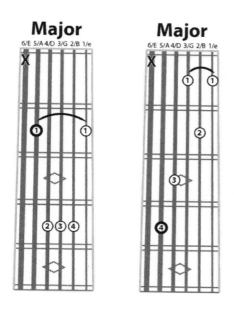

139

- or Min

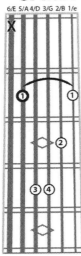

Sus or 4

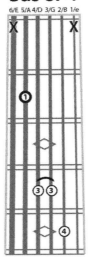

11,4 or Sus

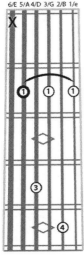

-7 or Min 7

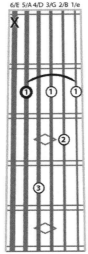

7 or Dom7

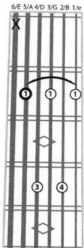

7 or Dom 7

Δ7 or Maj 7

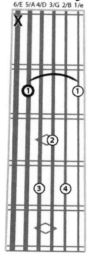

Δ7 or Maj 7

141

Dim

6/E 5/A 4/D 3/G 2/B 1/e

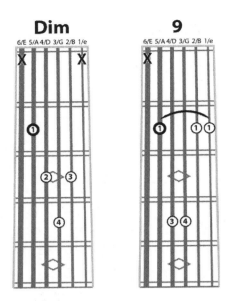

9

6/E 5/A 4/D 3/G 2/B 1/e

For some extra special "chord-construction goodness", check out the Chords section under the Lesson Menu at my website, ***www.yourguitarsage.com***

142

Chapter 25: The "CAGED" System

     The CAGED system is a great method for memorizing and visualizing chords on the fret board. Have you ever wanted to play a particular chord at a different place on the fret board? Did you know that you can play the same chord name in several different places on the guitar neck? Notice that the 1st 5 diagrams below are based off of chords C, A, G, E, D (open major chords). Each chord form below is a C major, however you can see that their shapes are based off of the open major chord forms C, A, G, E and D.

     By now you can see why we call this the CAGED system. Notice the last diagram showing all 5 chord forms overlapping on one fret board. This means that if a song called for a C chord, you could play any one of those forms below and it would sound good.

     The "1's" represent the tonic, key or root. In this case, the root is C. The "3's" and "5's" represent the 3rd and 5th scale notes of the major scale.

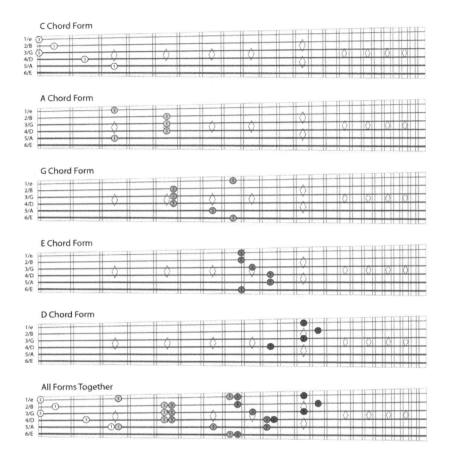

Practicing With the CAGED System

So now that you understand how the CAGED system works, just how can we practice it to make us better players? Before we go any further, I'd like to dissect this study into 2 parts: Concept and Fingering

Understanding the CAGED concept without picking up your guitar is Part 1 of this equation. That is to say, you should be able to understand the concept "on paper" before attempting to actually play the chords. Playing these chords fully or partially is yet a whole other story, but is our Part 2. That part will take a bit longer, but don't get discouraged! Remember, these are "open" chords that we will be attempting to assemble like bar chords. We don't have to play every note in the chord, but it's nice to know that we can if we should want or need to.

Firstly, you MUST know/memorize how to play the open chords of C, A, G, E and D. If you don't know how to do this already, you REALLY need to brush up on those chords before going any further. If you get any deeper without that knowledge, it will only confuse you. Knowing how the forms fall on the guitar neck is crucial to understanding and mapping the fret board. I use this knowledge dozens of times a day so rest assured that learning this new concept will revolutionize how you view the fret board.

Complete this chapter and you will understand the fret board better than a lot of other players out there today! Once the concept makes sense, (see the previous page and supplemental video in the directory) we can then tackle the fingering. I must emphasize that, although I show the entire chord, we don't have to play it in its entirety; in some cases it may be VERY inconvenient to do so.

So here is the method that I use myself to master these chords.

Play the open C chord. With all these chords make sure that each note that should be heard, IS heard. This will, of course, be easier for those that have had more time on the guitar. Now, for the "A" form of the C chord, lay your 1st finger across strings 5-1 (A through high E) at the 3rd fret. Make sure that your 1st finger is totally straight. For most people this means dropping the thumb down behind the neck so that the tip of your thumb is touching the bottom half of the neck. Unless you have Martian fingers, or are Jimi Hendrix, you most likely will not be able to hang your thumb over the top of the neck AND play a bar chord.

Trust me, learn it the right way and then "cheat" later if you master this technique. Okay, back to that "A" form. The 1st finger should be pressing down those 5 strings that I just mentioned. The rest of the bar can be played a couple of different ways; depending on the application, I use both. The first way you will play the 5th fret of strings 4, 3, and 2 with fingers 2, 3 and 4 (in that order). The other way is to play strings 4, 3 and 2 with finger 3 barred. The only way to get that high E to sound with this method is to hyper-extend the 3rd finger at the last knuckle (meaning bend it backwards a bit). Take your time! Slow and steady wins the race.

The G form is very tricky and difficult at first to play fully. First bar strings 4, 3 and 2 at the 5th fret with the 1st finger. Then, play string 5, fret 7 with the 2nd finger. Then string 6, fret 8 with the 3rd finger and finally the high E, fret 8 with the pinky. Getting cramps in your hand yet? You'll get it. The other way to play this chord is to play it partially – as I show in this video. Hang in there? Don't give up! This stuff takes time. <u>NO ONE</u> just gets it right away. Myth and ego say that one person can do this and not the other. Don't buy into it! You will be just as much a player as Hendrix or Stevie Ray IF you practice like they did.

Okay, so the "E" form is much easier. In fact, if you know how to play a full F chord (at the 1st fret), then you know how to play this chord already. Just "scootch" it up to the 8th fret! If you don't know the F, then place your 1st finger at the 8th fret and lay it across <u>all</u> 6 strings (just like on the "A" form, you must drop that thumb and get your hand out in front of the fret board a bit). Then place your 3rd finger on the A string at the 10th fret. Followed by the pinky on the D string at the 10th fret and the middle finger on the G string at the 9th fret. I'm purposely changing from string numbers to names (letters) because it's important that you know both.

Lastly, the "D" form is a little tricky. Place your 1st finger on the 10th fret of the D string. Then place the 2nd finger on the 12th fret of the G. Then place the 3rd finger on the 12th fret of the high E. Finally, place the pinky on the 13th fret of the B string. Now you are playing the "D" form of the C chord. Now let's do one more form because you are going to need it for keys other than C.

Since the "C" form of C is played open, we need to see what it would look like as a bar chord. So, for this example we are going to play a "C" form of the D chord. Place your pinky at the 5th fret of the A string. Then place the 3rd finger on the 4th fret of the D string. Place the 2nd finger on the 3rd fret of the B string. Finally, bar strings 1, 2 and 3 with the 1st finger at the 2nd fret. Now you have a movable C form. Get it?

Chapter 26: How to Play Guitar Tablature – Part 2

Previously in this book we learned the basics of tablature. Now that we understand that and have some other skills sets under our fingers and in our minds, let's further investigate this language of tablature.

Tablature Symbols

Remember how I said tablature provides a lot of detail? The following are tablature symbols that represent various techniques. Since new techniques are being discovered all the time, this is not an exhaustive list.

- h – hammer-on
- p – pull-off
- b – bend string
- / – slide up
- \ – slide down
- v – vibrato (sometimes written as ~)
- t – pick hand tap
- Harm– natural harmonic
- A.H.– artificial harmonic
- A.T. – tapped harmonic
- tr – trill
- T – tap
- TP or 3 diagonal lines under the note – tremelo picking
- PM – palm muting
- \n/ – tremolo bar dip; n = amount to dip
- \n – tremolo bar down
- n/ – tremolo bar up
- /n\ – tremolo bar inverted dip
- <> – volume swell (louder/softer)
- x – on rhythm slash represents muted slash

149

Hammer On

A "**hammer-on**" is a technique performed by sharply bringing a fretting-hand finger down on the fingerboard behind a fret causing a note to sound. For our example here, you would pick the fifth fret and hammer the seventh or eighth fret as indicated. Hammer-ons might feel awkward at first, but they are easily mastered with practice.

As the name indicates, hammer your finger in a quick snapping motion so that the string does not have time to fade out. A snappy hammer-on will vibrate the string almost as much as a strong picking.

By the way, this is the A minor pentatonic or C major pentatonic scale that you are about to play.

```
1st  string or e  ─────────────────── 5h8 ──────── thin string
2nd string or B  ──────────────── 5h8 ───────────
3rd string or G  ───────────── 5h7 ──────────────
4th string or D  ────────── 5h7 ─────────────────
5th string or A  ────── 5h7 ──────────────────────
6th string or E  ──── 5h8 ─────────────────── thick string
```

Pull-Off

A "**pull-off**" is the opposite of a hammer-on. A pull-off is a technique performed by plucking a string by "pulling" the string off the fingerboard with one of the fingers being used to fret the note. For our example here, you would pick the seventh or eighth fret as indicated and pull-off to the fifth fret. Pull-off s can also be a little awkward at first but with practice can be mastered. As its name indicates, pulling your finger off the fingerboard in a snapping motion causes the string to vibrate as if picked.

```
1st  string or e  ───────────────────8p5──────────  thin string
2nd string or B  ──────────────8p5──────────────
3rd  string or G  ─────────────7p5───────────────
4th  string or D  ──────────7p5──────────────────
5th  string or A  ──────7p5───────────────────────
6th  string or E  ───8p5──────────────────────────  thick string
```

Bend

A **bend** is represented by the symbol 'b' or an arrow bending up or down. A bend occurs when the guitarist physically pushes the string across the fret board causing a change in pitch. Since bends vary in duration and style, often times each arrow is illustrated differently. Often times, the word "full", or "1/2" will be written along with this, indicating that the note should be bent up either one whole-step or one half-step. Bends of larger intervals can occur. Typically the actual pitch change will be denoted.

```
1st  string or e  ─────────────────────────────────── thin string
2nd string or B  ─8b (full)─
3rd  string or G  ─────7b (1/2)─
4th  string or D  ───────────────────────────────────
5th  string or A  ───────────────────────────────────
6th  string or E  ─────────────────────────────────── thick string
```

Slide-Up/Slide-Down

A **slide-down** is represented by the
symbol "/". A slide-up occurs when a note is
picked and slid up to another note. The second
note is not picked, but instead is still vibrating
from the previous pick and the agitation of the
string during the slide. Opposite of a slide-up, a
slide-down is represented by the symbol '\'. A
slide- down occurs when a note is picked and
slid down to another note. Typically, mastering
the slide-down takes more time than mastering
the slide-up.

```
1st  string or e  ─────────────────────────────────── thin string
2nd string or B  ─7\5  7\5─
3rd  string or G  ───────5/7  5/7─
4th  string or D  ───────────────────────────────────
5th  string or A  ───────────────────────────────────
6th  string or E  ─────────────────────────────────── thick string
```

Vibrato

Vibrato is a pulsating effect by bending
the string in a rhythmic fashion. This technique
is created by bending the string up and down
rhythmically or shaking the string. This effect

works best after a string is picked. A vibrato is usually represented by 'v' or '~'.

```
1st  string or e ————————————————————————————————— thin string
2nd  string or B —————————————————————————————————
3rd  string or G ——⅄v————————————————————————————
4th  string or D ——————7————————————————————————
5th  string or A —————————————————————————————————
6th  string or E ————————————————————————————————— thick string
```

Tapping

The **tapping** technique is similar to a hammer-on, except it is done with the picking hand. It is almost always followed by a pull-off. The technique is performed when the picking hand taps the string hard enough to push the string against the fret creating a note to sound at that specific fret.

```
1st  string or e ————————————————————————————————— thin string
2nd  string or B —————————————————————————————————
3rd  string or G ——⅄—⅄—⅄—————————————————————————
4th  string or D —————————————————————————————————
5th  string or A —————————————————————————————————
6th  string or E ————————————————————————————————— thick string
```

Harmonic (Natural)

A **harmonic** is a "chimed" string. This technique is produced by plucking the string while lightly touching the string over the indicated fret. The fret is not actually played in the traditional sense. When done correctly, a chime-like sound will be produced.

Harmonic (Artificial)

Artificial harmonics are also known as a pseudo-harmonics, pinch-harmonics or "squealies." This technique requires allowing the string to lightly graze the side of your thumb after picking it. Don't try to over-think the process. When you pick a note, allow your thumb to keep traveling towards the string until it mutes it.

Once you get the hang of that, try letting the thumb just barely touch the string. If done properly, you will hear a slight chime. Pseudo-harmonics are typically easier to produce on lower pitched strings and lower fretted notes; however, if the proper technique is used, an artificial harmonic can be produced on any picked note.

Trill

The term "**trill**" is typically used when referring to a continuous back-and-forth, hammer-on and pull-off of two notes. Mastering the hammer-on and pull-off techniques will allow for quick and precise trills.

Tremolo Picking

Tremolo picking refers to fast, repetitive picking on one note. This technique is achieved by quickly picking a note up and down. Typically tremolo picking refers to single notes (not chords).

Palm Muting

Palm muting refers to the muting of strings with the picking hand in order to create a percussive or staccato (sharp attack) effect on notes or chords. This technique is achieved by placing the picking hand palm on the bridge of the guitar just where the strings meet the bridge. Backing the hand further towards the bridge creates a more standard, open sound. Moving the hand slightly closer to the strings will create a tighter, more closed-type sound. This technique can be used for all genres of music but is most prevalent in rock and heavy-metal rhythm guitar parts.

Tremolo Tricks

There could be a whole book written on this subject, but since most intricate tremolo work is done in hard rock/heavy metal music we won't be delving into the matter fully. Slash marks used for this notation direct the player to move the note down or up, or both in some fashion. Often times the targeted note will be denoted by the fret number, meaning that the designated fret number should be the desired pitch.

Volume Swell

This notation is used in tablature, musical notation and charts. An increase in volume is denoted by a "V" on its side like "<". A decrease in volume looks like the opposite ">". Changing the volume can obviously be done in numerous ways.

Chapter 27: Playing by Ear

Before we start learning how to play a song by ear, there are some things we need to define and explain:

Key: the tonality of a composition (song)

Chord: a simultaneous (at the same time) combination of at least three different pitches

Melody: a succession (series) of musical tones

Diatonic: the tones of a major or minor scale

Major Scale: a scale built from 2 whole steps, 1 half step, 3 whole steps, and 1 half step (or W W H W W W H)

99.9% of the time, the melody, chords, bass-lines, accompaniment, etc. will all be centered around one particular note or tonic. Some music is more tonal than others. Pop, blues, rock and country tend to be very stable in this regard. "Atonal" or "12 tone" music is on the extreme opposite end of this spectrum and we won't be studying it here. Think of the key as one particular note that all the other notes and chords dance around, point to or compliment. Every melody, bass line or chord progression that is played, points to a particular key. The key is like the title or idea of a song. If the title was, "Love Gone Wrong," your lyrics would probably be about a love that isn't going so hot. The lyrics would support the title. I know that sounds very elementary, but if you fully understand this concept it will help you TREMENDOUSLY.

Another example is if you had a report due, you would start with a thesis and all the other words, paragraphs and thoughts SHOULD support the thesis. If not, you would be considered to be "off the subject;" in musical terms you are falling out of the key.

So humor me for another moment yet...if your friends are sitting at a table talking about guitar and you pull up a chair and start talking about drums, things are going to get a little socially awkward. It's not to say that you could not reference drums as to how it might compare to guitars, but anything more than that and you are changing the subject. If your friends (the rest of the band or ensemble that you are playing with) decide not to change subjects (keys) with you, then you are going to be the odd man out, and YOU will be playing out of key. If you manage to get all those guitarists to start talking about drums, then you have managed to change the subject (key) for all your friends (band). Get it?

If you do reference drums and it pertains to the conversation regarding guitars, without intent of changing the subject, then musically we can do the same by suggesting another key temporarily without totally committing to that new key.

Often times a song will begin or end (or both) on the tonic, or "1" of the scale. This is often called the 1 chord, or 1 scale note.

Here is the method that I use when creating charts, melody lines, bass lines, or deciphering music by ear in any capacity:

1. Listen intently to a small part of the song you are trying to decipher.

Determining what melody or chords are being played will help you find what key the song is in. Finding out the key will make <u>unlocking</u> the rest of the song a breeze compared to NOT determining the key. It's the 1st thing that I always attempt to do when transcribing. You MUST be able to "hear" the note before trying to play it on your instrument. If I were to murmur something under my breath (that you can't accurately hear) and I ask you to repeat it, it would be a waste of time for you to guess at the infinite possibilities of what I COULD have said. So, normally you would ask me to repeat it, right? So when you are listening to a passage of music, you might need to listen to it over and over again until you can actually HEAR it accurately. Not being distracted by other noises (a friend trying to hum the melody or a T.V. on in the background, etc.) is also very important. I will even close my eyes so as to heighten my concentration on my aural sense (hearing) awareness. Hearing it right and playing it right are two TOTALLY different things so let's not rush this process.

The payoff for this learned skill is HUGE so don't give up, okay? The only thing that we are trying to do right now is hear, NOT play. Rushing this process WILL slow you down and hinder the "strengthening of your ear". If you feel you can't hear it correctly, try a smaller section of music, or use headphones or turn it up. Do something logical to get it "in your ears".

Once you feel sure that you are hearing the passage correctly, proceed to step two. (If you are having difficulties, keep pressing on. It's in EVERYONE to have this ability. Be patient with yourself and take it from someone who used to have a TERRIBLE ear...YOU CAN DO THIS!!!)

2. Hum the vocal melody-line, bass-line (or some other part of the song you are trying to decipher). Once I feel I can "hear" the music selection, I attempt to hum it. This is a learned skill! I say this because some say that it is a gift (which is TOTALLY false and assumes a LOT of things). However, you will find that the more you practice, the better you get. Coincidence? Now the fun part! This can be a bit tricky if you are not used to humming or singing. The trick is to commit to the note that you are humming until you can successfully find it on your guitar. Take the first note of the series of notes and hum it – LOUD AND PROUD! That first note is crucial. If you are not convinced that you have the note, slide (sing it up and down in pitch) until you get it. Be aware/focused and limit distractions, especially other noises. NOW that you have hummed the note correctly...

3. Find the note on the fret board.

How? Go fish! Yup, just play a note on

the fret board, preferably in a place on the neck you think is logical. You probably won't be WAY up on the neck unless it's a high melody. If you don't luck out and get the note right off the bat, determine if the note that you are humming is higher or lower than the note being played. ATTENTION: This is the most important part of the puzzle with the exception of hearing the note correctly in step 1. You MUST determine the "highness" or "lowness" of the two pitches. This is where most people bail out, and try going back a step or going forward a step. Don't do it! It will only slow you down. This is the normal process for everyone in some capacity or another. Once you have determined that the played note is higher or lower than the hummed note, move your played note in the direction of your hummed note BY HALF STEPS (1 fret at a time). For example, if your hummed note is higher than your played note on the guitar, then you would move your played note UP by half steps slowly until the note is in unison (the same). For beginners, try moving up in half steps on 1 string. If you are not trained, changing strings will only confuse you.

If you don't find that first benchmark note, the other notes will be much harder to find, so don't skip any steps in this process. It seems tedious, but the more you do this the quicker you'll get. Whether you are really slow at this in the beginning or get REALLY quick over time, the process is the same. Like a speed-typist, the speed comes from methodically doing the correct steps EVERY time, not randomly doing some steps and hoping for a good outcome. That's called "dum" and that's not you. Yeah, I know I spelled it without the "b." Just making sure you are paying attention! And without the "b" it's EXTRA stupid. Gotcha again!

4. Find more notes on the fret board.

So once you get that first note, half the battle is done. Use the same method above to find the other notes. Another great practice is to take small "chunks" of music at a time. Like eating a meal, you don't take more than you can chew or swallow, so don't do that with musical passages, okay?

5. Determine the key.

The combination of whole steps and half steps will determine where your tonic or "1" is. Now, assuming you have a few notes that you have successfully "found" on the fret board due to your stellar humming skills, what do you do with them? Well, we are looking for a pattern, specifically the major scale. If you remember, the major scale pattern is WWHWWWH (whole-step, whole-step, half-step, whole-step, whole-step, whole-step, half-step) or (1 W 2 W 3 H 4 W 5 W 6 W 7 H 1) - where the numbers are the scale steps. A half-step remember, is the distance between one fret and the next. A whole-step is two half-steps.

SO, let's say the 3 notes that you have found show a pattern of WWH. DEAR WATSON, a clue or three to be exact!! Here is where that WWH falls into our little major scale pattern from above: 1 W 2 W 3 H 4 W 5 W 6 W 7 H

Get it? So, in our example, there are **two places** that that pattern falls, so we are closer, but no cigar just yet. You are the detective and are looking for clues as to what key we are in. The song has the "fingerprints and DNA" of the key we are looking for, ALL OVER IT, but we have to look carefully, and jumping to conclusions could give us wrong answers. We need to get more notes from the song to determine where the "1" from the scale is. Let's say after further listening, humming and translating our hummed notes to the guitar, we find that the pattern now has a W before the initial WWH to create WWWH. Voila!! NOW, we are getting somewhere! Now we have WWWH and notice how there is only one of those in the following pattern: 1 W 2 W 3 H 4 W 5 W 6 W 7 H 1. That means that the note at the end of the WWWH would be the 1, tonic or key of the song. That is HUGE to know and I will show you why.

Once we have determined the key, we have a matrix of very possible chords and notes that will coincide with that particular key (the Nashville Number System chord matrix and major scale are examples of this). So for example, let's say after using the above method and determining that our song is in the key of C. Our chord "subset" or family of chords would MOST LIKELY be: C, D-, E-, F, G, A- and B dim (diminished). I say most likely, because it's not always the case, BUT it's a great place to start. Your ear will most likely tell you if a chord is different from that "rule of thumb" set of chords.

So now that we know that these are the most probable chords that we should expect to see in our example song, we are not just grabbing chords randomly. Often times, that 7 chord WON'T be diminished, but will be a "flat 7" chord. So in the key of C, the B diminished would be a Bb Major. See what we did there? We flattened the B by one half-step, making it a

165

Bb. Then we built a major chord off that Bb. Remember the "flat 7" chord. You will see it A LOT in pop, rock and country music.

As a side thought, when I am teaching my one-on-one students a song, I almost always pull up the video online. Often times, videos will show the artist as they are playing their guitars. Since the guitar is so versatile, the same melody or chord progression might have 3 or 4 possible solutions (ways to play it) on the neck. So it's helpful to notice where or if a capo is used, or where on the neck the guitarist is playing. This will all make more sense to you as you gradually learn this process.

6. Hum the bass notes to find your chord progression.

Using the above methods, once I have determined the key and have the subset of probable chords and notes, I listen to the bass notes. When I refer to the bass notes, I mean those notes that are played by the bass player or are in the lowest register of the composition. Basically, I am listening to the lowest notes (in pitch). 9 times out of 10, the bass notes will tell you what the letter name of the chord is.

Now mind you, there are many different

methods people use to transcribe music by ear. The way that I'm showing you is one way, and for me is the easiest and most logical way. As you sharpen your own aural-awareness, you will most likely develop your own techniques and habits that are unique to you.

Let's say for our example, that we hear the bass line play a C for 4 beats, a G for 4 beats, an A for 4 beats and an F for 4 beats. Remember our melody determined that we were in the key of C and that the associated chords for that key are C, D-, E-, F, G, A- and B dim (diminished). Remember that the bass note is only one note of the chord and does not determine the "flavor" of the chord like major, minor, diminished, 7th etc. So the four bass notes that we found, C, G, A and F would most likely represent chords C major, G major, A minor and F major. Could it be that the chords that are actually played in the song are different than that? Sure, but most likely not. They usually fit the matrix of the key that we are in.

The method that I just showed you was how I taught myself how to transcribe songs. For those of you just starting out, I would suggest going through each step. If you are finding success skipping some of these steps, then more power to you! However, *if you are having difficulty*, do them all. This is an incredible skill to develop and will SERIOUSLY revolutionize your playing. All of my students are different. Each comes with a unique skill set and way of learning. Now, when I sit down to transcribe a song for a student, I will usually jump straight to step 6 where I am humming the bass notes. From doing this process so much, I can usually determine what the tonic of the song is right away. Finding my bass notes tells me my chord progression and also tells me where I might put my capo to simplify the song.

Again, let me remind you that this is a learned skill. I hate even saying that one person might be naturally better at this than another because I don't want to give you an excuse to not learn this skill. It can be frustrating at first but if you are persistent, the rewards are great and every time you find a new note and new chord it's like finding a piece of gold. It's always helpful to start with a song that you are very familiar with and that you love. It will make this whole process a lot easier and more enjoyable.

Also, remember, regarding guitar and anything associated with art in general, there is no perfect way. It's all subjective and open to interpretation. I'm not saying that there are not definite notes or chords represented in the song, but that your method for determining those may be different than someone else's. Always be open to learning. In this way, you will always be increasing in skill and not grow stagnant.

Chapter 28: Introduction to Chord Construction

As defined in the <u>Diatonic Harmony</u> chapter, a chord is 3 or more notes played at the same time. Let me add a bit more detail for the real world. The most basic type of chord is a 3 note chord, called a triad. Usually, those three notes are different notes. Don't make the mistake of assuming this means how many fingers are holding down notes for your chord. For example, an E minor chord only utilizes 2 fingers while still sounding 3 or more notes. I happen to run into this a lot with new students, which is why I mention it.

With every chord there is a root. The root is the letter name of the chord (i.e.-A, B, C#), and the one note on which the rest of the chord is built upon. For instance, C major and A major have the same formula – which categorizes both as major chords - but since that formula is calculated from 2 different roots (A and C), then 2 different chords are produced.

In this section, we will discuss the 4 basic triad types (major, minor, diminished, and augmented). All chords are analyzed and named according to the notes (or better yet, the intervals) that they contain. An interval is the distance between 2 notes. These notes, or interval distances, are all derived from the major scale. In order to build or embellish chords from scratch, one must have a good working knowledge of the major scale, it's formula of whole-step, whole-step, half-step, whole-step, whole-step, whole-step, half-step (WWHWWWH) and the scale step names (1, 2, 3, 4, 5, 6, 7, 8 or 1). Also, remember that when we sharpen (#) a note, we raise it one 1/2 step, and when we flatten (b) a note, we lower it one 1/2 step.

Please note the following formulas, as you will need them as we continue.

Major chord (1, 3, 5): a major chord consists of the 1st, 3rd and 5th scale steps of the major scale. The distance between the 1st and 3rd notes is 2 whole-steps. The distance between the 3rd and 5th notes is 1 and 1/2 steps.

Minor chord (1, b3, 5): a minor chord consists of the 1st, flat 3rd and 5th scale steps of the major scale. The distance between the 1st and 3rd notes is 1 and 1/2 steps. The distance between the 3rd and 5th notes is 2 whole-steps. This means that any major chord you know can easily be converted to a minor chord by flatting the 3rd, or lowering it by a half-step (1 fret). If you already know your E major and E minor chords, notice that the only thing that changes between the 2 chords is the 1st finger. When that 1st finger is pressed down (on the 1st fret of the 3rd string), it's sounding the 3rd of the scale. When the finger is released the string is played open and the flatted 3rd is sounded.

Another example is the A major and A minor chord. Notice the difference between the 2 chords. There is only 1 note that changes between the 2 and that takes place on the 2nd string when the C# is flattened by a half-step making the note a C which changes the chord from major to minor. Since there is only 1 note that changes from both chord examples that we just used (E minor and A minor), we can assume that all the other notes are ones and fives.

Let's try another example. Play a D major and then play a D minor. Notice that the only note that changes is on the first string, where the F# is flattened to an F to make the chord minor. Again we can assume that all the other notes in this chord are ones and fives because the only thing that changes between the major and minor chord is the third.

Diminished chord (1, b3, b5): a diminished chord consists of the 1st, flatted 3rd and flatted 5th scale steps of the major scale. The distance between the 1st and 3rd steps is 1 and ½ steps. The distance between the 3rd and 5th steps is 1 and 1/2 steps. Since the only difference between the minor chord and the diminished chord is the 5th scale step, it's simple to convert any minor chord into a diminished chord by simply flatting any "fifths" that occur in the chord. For example, play a D minor chord. Your 2nd finger should be playing the 2nd fret of the 3rd string. That note is the only 5th in a D minor chord, so lowering it by half-step or one fret will change that chord to a D diminished chord. In order to play this chord properly you will most likely need to bar the 1st three strings with your 1st finger on the 1st fret while your 3rd finger plays the 3rd fret of the 2nd string.

Augmented chord (1, 3, #5): an augmented chord consists of the 1st, 3rd and sharpened 5th scale steps of the major scale. The distance between the 1st and 3rd steps is 2 whole-steps. The distance between the 3rd and 5th steps is also 2 whole-steps. Since the only difference between the major chord and the augmented chord is the 5th scale step, it's simple to convert any major chord to an augmented chord by simply sharpening any "fifths" that occur in the chord. For example, play a D major chord. Do you remember where the 5th is from our last example? That's right, the 2nd fret of the 3rd string.

So the only thing we need to do to change this major chord to an augmented chord is raise the 5th by a half step or 1 fret. I'm not going to help you out on the fingering of this one. You are growing in your skills and sometimes you won't have instruction to rely on. So use your intuition and common sense to discover a fingering for this new chord that is logical and playable for you. There is no right answer per se. There may be more logical answers for this type of thing however.

Being equipped with these 4 formulas and a movable major scale will allow you to create literally hundreds of chord forms across the guitar neck. For the intermediate and advanced guitar player this is where we start upping our game. I use these formulas all the time when formulating guitar parts for studio or live performance.

Now for the exercise portion of the program!

Strum an open G major chord. Now use any of the major scale formulas that I have provided to determine which scale step each of the notes of the G major chord represents. Basically, we are looking for the scale degree number, not the letter name of the notes. For instance, slowly strum or Arpeggiate the G major chord from the 6th string to the 1st string.

Now play a G major scale. The 1st or lowest note of the G major chord is obviously the 1st note of the G major scale, so this note would be a "one", or the "one" of the chord. Play the next note which should be a "B" on the 5th string. Now play through your G major scale saying out loud each number of the scale as you play it and stop at that B note. The number that you are saying when you land on the "B" should be "3", making that note the "3" of the chord. Get it? Now continue on with this same technique to determine the scale step of every note in the G chord.

You will need to use your ear to compare and contrast notes as the scale form may not always exactly match where the notes of your chord fall. For instance, the 5th scale step of the G major (form 1) scale is a "D", which will be played by the pinky on the 5th fret of the 5th string. However, we are looking to identify the open 4th string (D string). If your guitar is tuned correctly, the D on the 5th fret of the A string should sound identical to the open 4th string. If you have not used this technique before, you really need to get familiar with it as it is used very frequently in the discovery of notes on your fret board.

At first this can be tricky, but don't give up! The payoff is huge in regards to mastering your fret board. Once you have all the scale steps identified in the G chord, start moving on to your other open chords. Remember that you must use the associated major scale with the chord that you are analyzing. For instance, if you are analyzing a C major chord, you must use a C major scale. If you are analyzing an A minor chord, you must use an A major scale. Don't forget that the major scale is our cornerstone for all analysis when it comes to music. We refer to it frequently, so it's extremely important that you know it inside and out. Once you master this technique you are going to start looking at chords in a totally different way and it will truly empower your playing abilities.

Now go rock some new chords!

Chapter 29: Building Seventh Chords

There is an expression that says, "Give a man a fish and he eats for a day, teach a man to fish and he eats for a lifetime." <u>That is to say</u>, if I show you a chord and show you where to put your fingers on what frets, you could memorize the chord easily. But if I show you how to assemble chords from scratch, then I enable you for years to come. There are literally thousands of chords. So it's your choice: memorize each chord or learn a method of assembling them and save yourself hundreds of hours. How cool would it be if I could show you how to make a seventh chord out of every chord that you already know instead of having to memorize hundreds of chords, effectively doubling or tripling your chord vocabulary in one night? If your answer was anything close to "Super-uber-mega-cool!!!," then HANG ON, because we are getting ready to rock!

As a rule, shortcuts typically "cut" some stuff out and often times "short" you of the full picture. But you know that already, and that's why you are studying so diligently. So digesting this information, understanding the concept and putting it into practice may take extra time up front (the long way), but I promise you it won't take you nearly the amount of time it would take you to memorize a few hundred new chords (the "shortcut").

The definition of a seventh chord is a chord consisting of a triad plus a note forming an interval of a seventh above the chords root. There are seven commonly used seventh chords in Western music. You can easily master these first 3 (most often used) formulas - immediately doubling your minor chord vocabulary and tripling your major chord vocabulary. How cool is that? Take your time with these and get the first three formulas down before moving to the others (FYI-The three most popular formulas are Major 7th, Minor 7th and Dominant 7th.)

Major seventh - for example Dmaj7, DM7, DΔ, etc. (these are chord symbols that you will see on charts)

Formation -(1, 3, 5, 7): to easily convert any major chord into a major seventh chord, find a higher octave of the root and flatten it by a half-step (meaning, don't flat the lowest note - the root, but find a higher octave to alter). For example, play a D major chord. To convert this chord to a D major seventh, drop the high D on the second string back one half-step to Db (or C#). To play this easily, bar the second fret at strings 1, 2 and 3 while you play the 4th string open.

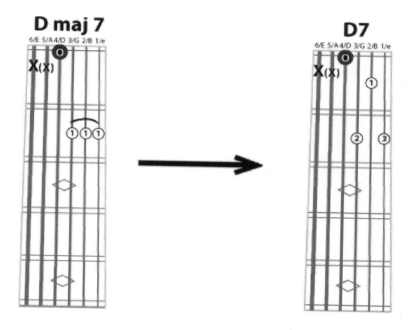

Minor seventh - for example Emin7, Em7, E-7, etc.

Formation - (1, b3, 5, b7): to easily convert any minor chord into a minor seventh chord, find a higher octave of the root and flatten it by one whole-step. For example, play an E minor chord. To convert this chord to an E minor seventh, drop the E on the fourth string

179

back one whole-step to the open D. Then strum all the strings.

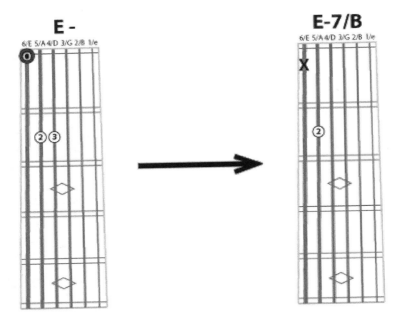

Dominant seventh - for example A7 or A7

Formation - (1, 3, 5, b7): to easily convert any major chord into a dominant seventh chord, find a higher octave of the root and flatten it by 1 whole-step. For example, play an A major chord. To convert this chord to an A dominant seventh, drop the A on the 3rd string back one whole-step to the open G. Then strum strings 1 through 5.

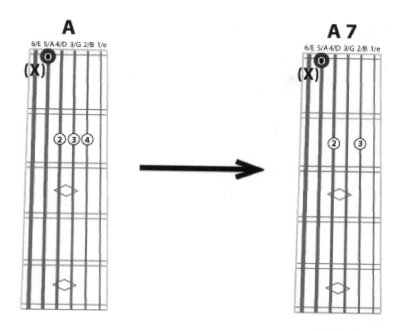

Half-diminished seventh - for example "D minor seventh flat five" Dm7b5, D-7b5, etc.

Formation - (1, b3, b5, b7): to easily convert any minor seventh chord into a half-diminished seventh chord, flatten the 5 by a half-step. For example, play a D minor seventh chord. To convert this chord to a D half diminished seventh chord, flatten the A on the 2nd fret of the 3rd string by a half-step, to an Ab (or G#). This chord can easily be played by barring strings 1-3 at the 1st fret and strumming strings 1-4.

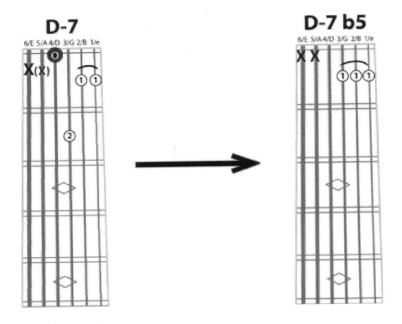

Diminished seventh - for example D°7, or Ddim7

Formation - (1, b3, b5, bb7 (or 6 - known as enharmonic 6)): to easily convert any half-diminished seventh chord to a diminished seventh chord, flatten again the already b7. On the above D half-diminished seventh chord that we just played, flatten the C (on the second string) by a half-step. The fretting should be as follows high E string (1st fret), B string (open), G string (1st fret), D string (open). Now, if you are anything like me, that double-flat seven (bb7) bothers you. This is how it is justified. These are 7th chords we are talking about right? How can a 7th chord NOT have a 7 (interval) in it, but a 6 instead? Things get a little complicated with this type if theory, but no worries! I will guide you through it. Too, I don't expect you to digest/retain all of this in one sitting. It may take several days or weeks for this to really settle in, depending on how much attention you give it. Let's keep moving forward.

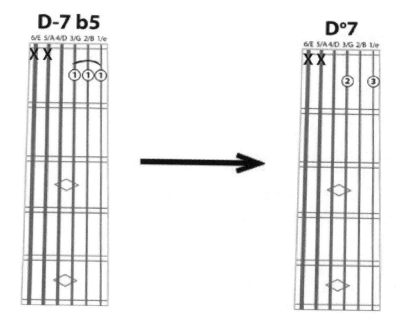

Minor major seventh- for example Dmmaj7, DmM7, DmΔ7, D-Δ7, etc.

Formation - (1, b3, 5, 7): to easily convert any major seventh chord to a minor major seventh chord (I know "minor major" right? Just roll with it.); flatten the third by a half-step. For instance, play the D major seventh chord from our 1st example. Now flatten the 3 which is on the second fret of the first string. If you move this one note back one half-step to the "F", it will produce a D minor major seventh chord.

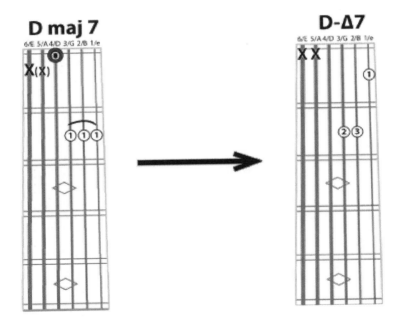

Augmented major seventh - for example Dmaj7(#5), D+M7, D+Δ7, etc.

Formation - (1, 3, #5, 7): to easily convert any major 7th chord to an augmented major 7th chord; sharpen the 5th by a half-step. For instance, play a D major seventh chord. Now find the 5th and raise it by a half-step. The D string should be played open, while the 3rd string is fretted at the 3rd fret, and strings 1 and 2 are fretted at the 2nd fret.

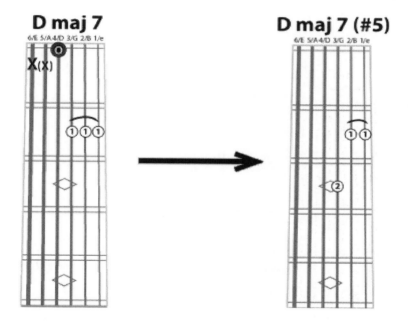

Whew!!! Now go take a rest! I know your brain is tired! Mine sure is! Remember to take this slow. You could no more easily digest all of this than you could an entire Thanksgiving meal! But over time, this will be no problem.

Remember, I can easily say "this is this chord, and that is that chord," but that won't make your brain start thinking - which is what I am trying to do here with you. If this feels like too much for you at one time, try to understand the concepts on the first 3 examples. Those are the ones that you are going to use the most. Dominant seventh chords are very popular in blues and other styles of music, so if you like blues make sure that you understand dominant sevenths. If you're interested in learning jazz guitar, it will be important that you eventually learn all of these examples. Now go grab your guitar and start applying these concepts immediately so that they can become part of your playing.

Thank you for all your support! Please leave your feedback by leaving your book review. Thanks in advance! Go visit:
www.yourguitarsage.com/book-review

Summary

WOW, you made it!!! Not just through this book, but through understanding some of the most important subjects in regards to guitar. I have been playing for nearly 30 years and know MANY guitar players that have been playing that long that don't know many of these concepts. SOO, it really is a big deal that you have made it this far.

All of these concepts, ideas, definitions and exercises were designed to give you more "colors" in your palette. <u>YOU</u> are the artist! Don't let anything that you have learned here or from anywhere else hinder your art. It's NOT about rules! However, all these bits and pieces are going to help you decipher the code of music. They will allow you to play new parts that you would not have thought of before, had you not stretched your mind.

Everyone has different goals and different skills that they bring to the table, including YOU. Don't be discouraged about what another can do "better" than you. You have your own skills and goals. You are unique! I can't express that enough! If everyone was a virtuoso speed player, guitar would be very boring. EVERYONE has a place in the musical spectrum. SOO, practice and use what you are going to use for YOUR goals and forget the rest. You can always come back to it and refresh your memory. Having taken the time to go through the whole regimen however will allow you to KNOW what you need and what you don't. Plus, it will just make you a better musician overall.

I'm proud of you! I want to hear from you and about your accomplishments on this beautiful and exciting instrument called the guitar. Send me pics, send me stories, and let your friends know of the lessons. I plan on teaching 50 years from now, so I'm not going anywhere. Stick with me and I'll stick with you!

And remember the final and most IMPORTANT of all the lessons: Practice, practice, practice!!

Thank You

Before you go I would like to say a big "thank you" for purchasing and reading my book.

I know you could have easily purchased someone else's book on guitar lessons and how to play the guitar. But you took a chance with my book.

Huge thanks for purchasing this book and finishing the entire book.

If you liked this book then I need your help real quick!

Please take a few moments to leave a review for this book on Amazon: **http://www.yourguitarsage.com/book-review**

Your feedback will continue to help me provide you and everyone else with more guitar books. And if you really liked it then please let me know :)

One Last Thing My Friend...

If you feel like other people could benefit from the material that is in this book then feel free to share it with your friends.

Thanks again!

http://www.facebook.com/yourguitarsage

http://www.twitter.com/yourguitarsage

A Cause Close to My Heart

As many of you know, I am a BIG animal lover and advocate for animal welfare. I also believe to be of great significance in this world, we need to leave more than we have taken and we MUST take a stand for those that don't have a voice. Two things that I have always been passionate about are guitars and animals. If you have a heart for animals like I do, you will be happy to know that a portion of every YourGuitarSage purchase is given to animal welfare organizations like: **www.NoKillAdvocacyCenter.org** and **www.TribeOfHeart.org**.

Many people have not taken the time to understand the gravity or plight of many of the animals living in our world today. Since the cause is so big, I have focused my cause on the issues of "spay and neuter" and animal cruelty prevention through legislation, law enforcements and education. "Spay and neuter" is also known as animal population control or the sterilization of domesticated (house) pets and feral (wild) animals where necessary and able. It's a simple procedure that can save millions of animals' lives every year from the carelessness/cruelty of humans (a supposed "higher" life form). Here are some basic facts to show you just how quickly one cat or dog left to breed can have a DRASTIC impact on the death toll.

Cat		Dog	
1st year	3 litters = 12 offspring	1st year	4 offspring with 2 females
2nd year	144 offspring	2nd year	12 offspring
3rd year	1,728 offspring	3rd year	36 offspring
4th year	10,736 offspring	5th year	324 offspring

If you are a pet owner, I IMPLORE you to spay/neuter your animal. This is an EASY way to change 1000s of innocent lives. Oh yeah, and Karma will shine upon you :)

Also, if you feel moved to do so, please give to the organizations above. Together, we have the power to change this world! *Please join me!*

Resources

Your Guitar Sage Website

www.yourguitarsage.com

Free Online Guitar Lessons

www.unstoppableguitarsystem.com

YourGuitarSage YouTube Channel: 100s of Free Songs and Technique Videos

www.youtube.com/yourguitarsage

Beginners Technique Videos

www.yourguitarsage.com/beginners-technique

Facebook

www.facebook.com/yourguitarsage

Twitter

www.twitter.com/yourguitarsage

The Guitar Blog

www.yourguitarsage.com/blog

Gear Questions

www.yourguitarsage.com/faqs/guitar-gear/

Free Tablature Paper

www.yourguitarsage.com/printable-blank-guitar-tablature-paper

Anatomy of the Guitar

www.yourguitarsage.com/anatomy-of-the-guitar

Posture

www.yourguitarsage.com/posture

Dexterity

www.yourguitarsage.com/dexterity

How to Tune Your Guitar

www.yourguitarsage.com/tune-guitar

How to Play Open Chords

www.yourguitarsage.com/open-chords

Talent vs. Practice

www.yourguitarsage.com/talent-practice

Strumming Method

www.yourguitarsage.com/strumming-method

Master ANY Strumming Rhythm

www.yourguitarsage.com/master-guitar-strumming

Number System Chart – Cover Song Example

www.yourguitarsage.com/nashville-system-chart

How to Use a Capo

www.yourguitarsage.com/capo

Basics to Fingerpicking

www.yourguitarsage.com/basics-fingerpicking

Cover Song Example on Fingerpicking

www.yourguitarsage.com/cover-song-fingerpicking

Harpsichord Technique

www.yourguitarsage.com/harpsichord-technique

Expand Your Knowledge to Notes on the Fretboard

www.yourguitarsage.com/notes-fretboard

Springboards

www.yourguitarsage.com/springboards

Diatonic Harmony

www.yourguitarsage.com/diatonic-harmony

6th 5th String Root Major Scales

www.yourguitarsage.com/major-scales-6th-5th-string-root

5th String Root 2 Octave – Major Scale

www.yourguitarsage.com/2-octave-major-scale-5th-string-root

6th String Root 2 Octave – Major Scale

www.yourguitarsage.com/2-octave-major-scale-6th-string-root

Single String Major Scale

www.yourguitarsage.com/single-string-major-scale

The Power of the Pentatonic Scale

www.yourguitarsage.com/pentatonic-scale

Form 1 A min and C maj – Pentatonic Scale

www.yourguitarsage.com/form-1-a-minor-c-major

Chord Noodling Improvisation

www.yourguitarsage.com/chord-noodling-improvisation

Blues Improvisation – Call and Response

www.yourguitarsage.com/call-and-response

Chord Noodling Part 1

www.yourguitarsage.com/chord-noodling-part-1

Chord Noodling Part 2

www.yourguitarsage.com/chord-noodling-part-2

How to Play Suspension Chords and Some Fancy Chord Noodling

www.yourguitarsage.com/suspension-chords

Cover Example – Chord Noodling

www.yourguitarsage.com/cover-chord-noodling

Over 300 Bar Chords

Part 1: www.yourguitarsage.com/bar-chords-part-1

Part 2: www.yourguitarsage.com/bar-chords-part-2

12 Bar Blues

www.yourguitarsage.com/12-bar-blues

The "effing F Chord

www.yourguitarsage.com/effing-f-chord

The "CAGED" System

www.yourguitarsage.com/caged-system

Building Seventh Chords

www.yourguitarsage.com/building-seventh-chords

Amazon.com Bestseller - Ukulele Mastery Simplified

www.ukulelemasterysimplified.com

Thank you for all your support! Please leave your feedback by leaving your book review. Thanks in advance! Go visit:
www.yourguitarsage.com/book-review

Do you need help with learning the guitar? Check out my free video course on how to quickly master both your fretting and strumming hand. Visit www.unstoppableguitarsystem.com today.

Printed in Poland
by Amazon Fulfillment
Poland Sp. z o.o., Wrocław